THE CUBANS

Other books in the
Coming to America series:

COMING TO AMERICA

THE CUBANS

Jacquelyn Landis, *Book Editor*

Bruce Glassman, *Vice President*
Bonnie Szumski, *Publisher*
Helen Cothran, *Managing Editor*

GREENHAVEN PRESS
An imprint of Thomson Gale, a part of The Thomson Corporation

Detroit • New York • San Francisco • San Diego • New Haven, Conn.
Waterville, Maine • London • Munich

For more information, contact
Greenhaven Press
27500 Drake Rd.
Farmington Hills, MI 48331-3535
Or you can visit our Internet site at http://www.gale.com

Cover credit: © David Young-Wolff/Photo Edit. A Cuban American couple dances to music performed by a traditional Salsa band.

LIBRARY OF CONGRESS CATALOGING-IN-PUBLICATION DATA

The Cubans / Jacquelyn Landis, book editor.
  p. cm. — (Coming to America)
Includes bibliographical references and index.
ISBN 0-7377-2763-2 (lib. : alk. paper)
  1. Cuban Americans—History. 2. Cuban Americans—Social conditions.
3. Immigrants—United States—History. 4. Refugees—United States—History.
5. Cuba—Emigration and immigration—History. 6. United States—Emigration
and immigration—History. 7. Cuban Americans—Biography. I. Landis, Jacquelyn.
II. Coming to America (San Diego, Calif.)
E184.C97C845 2005
973'.04687291—dc22
                                             2004060583

Printed in the United States of America

Contents

Chapter 1: The Early Cuban Exiles

Chapter 2: Political Unrest and the Next Waves of Immigration

Chapter 3: The Refugee Crisis and How It Changed Life in the United States

integrating being both Cuban and American, and sometimes feel caught between the two.

Chapter 4: The Accomplishments of Cuban Americans

FOREWORD

In her popular novels, such as *The Joy Luck Club* and *The Bonesetter's Daughter*, Chinese American author Amy Tan explores the complicated cultural and social differences between Chinese-born mothers and their American-born daughters. For example, the mothers eat foods and hold religious beliefs that their daughters either abhor or abstain from, while the daughters pursue educational and career opportunities that were not available to the previous generation. Generation gaps occur in almost all families, but as Tan's writings show, such differences are even more pronounced when parents grow up in a different country. When immigrants come to the United States, their initial goal is often to start a new life that is an improvement from the life they experienced in their homeland. However, while these newcomers may intend to fully adapt to American culture, they inevitably bring native customs with them. Immigrants have helped make America broader culturally by introducing new religions, languages, foods, and different ways of looking at the world. Their children and subsequent generations, however, often seek to cast aside these traditions and instead more fully absorb mainstream American mores.

As Tan's writings suggest, the dissimilarities between immigrants and their children are manifested in several ways. Adults who come to the United States and do not learn English turn to their children, educated in the American school system, to serve as interpreters and translators. Children, seeing what their American-born schoolmates eat, reject the foods of their native land. Religion is another area where the generation gap is particularly pronounced. For example, the liturgy of Syrian Christian services had to be translated into English when most young Syrian Americans no longer knew how to speak Syriac. Numerous Jews, freed from the European ghettos they had lived in, wished to assimilate more fully into the surrounding culture and began to loosen the traditional dietary and ritual requirements under which they had grown up. Reformed Judaism, which began in Germany, thus found a strong foothold among young Jews born in America.

However, no generational experiences have been as significant as that between immigrant mothers and their daughters. Living in the United States has afforded girls and young women opportunities they likely would not have had in their homelands. The daughters of immigrants, in some cases, live entirely different lives than their mothers did in their native nations. Where an Arab mother may have only received a limited education, her American-raised daughter enjoys a full course of American public schooling, often continuing on to college and careers. A woman raised in India might have been placed in an arranged marriage, while her daughter will have the opportunity to date and choose a husband. Admittedly, not all families have been willing to give their daughters all these new freedoms, but these American-born girls are frequently more willing to declare their wishes.

The generation gap is only one aspect of the immigrant experience in the United States. Understanding immigrants' unique and shared experiences and their contributions to American life is an interesting way to study the many people who make up the American citizenry. Greenhaven Press's Coming to America series helps readers learn why more people have moved to the United States than to any other nation. Selections on the lives of immi-

grants once they have reached America, from their struggles to find employment to their experiences with discrimination and prejudice, help give students insights into
stereotypes and cultural mores that continue to this day.
Finally, profiles of prominent immigrants help the reader
become aware of the many achievements of these people
in fields ranging from science to politics to sports.

Each volume in the Coming to America series takes an
extensive look into a particular immigrant population. The
carefully selected primary and secondary sources provide
both historical perspectives and firsthand insights into the
immigrant experience. Combined with an in-depth intro-
duction and a comprehensive chronology and bibliogra-
phy, every book in the series is a valuable addition to the
study of American history. With immigrants comprising
nearly 12 percent of the U.S. population, and their children and grandchildren constantly adding to the population, the immigrant experience continues to evolve. Coming to America is consequently a beneficial tool for not
only understanding America's past but also its future.

INTRODUCTION

The United States has many immigrant communities, pockets of foreign-born residents who tend to gather in the same geographic areas during their early days in the country. After immigrants have lived in the country for a while, they usually begin to spread out to other areas, pursuing opportunity, joining other family members, or simply satisfying their curiosity. The Cuban American community has resisted this pattern, remaining primarily in Florida. The 2000 U.S. Census counted 1.24 million Cubans and Cuban descendants living in the country. Two-thirds reside in Florida, with the overwhelming majority in South Florida. The population of Miami alone is one-third Cuban American.

Several reasons explain the Cuban Americans' reluctance to leave Florida. Following the 1959 revolution in Cuba, when Fidel Castro's forces overthrew the government of Fulgencio Batista, thousands of Cubans fled the country, fearing persecution from Castro's new government. Once they were safely in the United States, they considered themselves exiles rather than immigrants. That belief has not changed much over the years: Many Cuban Americans still cling to the belief that their exile is temporary and that one day they will be able to return to their homeland. Only ninety miles separate Cuba from Florida, and perhaps the physical closeness inspires a psychological closeness to home. If the exiles are permitted to return to Cuba when Fidel Castro is no longer in power, the short distance will be easily navigable.

Another reason Cuban Americans have resisted leaving Florida is that the concentration of so many Cubans in a relatively small area—Little Havana in Miami, for example—allows them to preserve their culture and customs to an extent rarely rivaled by other immigrant groups. It is entirely possible for a Cuban American to live, work, and play within the confines of Little Havana without ever leaving the neighborhood or having to speak a word of English. Although it is common for immigrant groups to gravitate together in their communities, few immigrant communities have produced such a cohesive self-contained community.

Perhaps the most important reason the Cuban American community has stuck together is the unprecedented political power and influence the exiles have amassed. Soon after their arrival they discovered that they had power in numbers. From the early days just after the revolution, the exiles have adamantly taken a hard-line stance in opposition to Castro. Because of their sheer numbers they have been able to influence elections in Florida, supporting candidates who agree with their anti-Castro position. Furthermore, because Florida is usually a battleground state in national elections, that influence has spread to presidential elections as well. Those in the Cuban American community who are determined to achieve their goal of toppling Castro would be unwilling to dilute their power by relocating to other parts of the country.

It is unusual for this kind of cohesive resolve—a resolve both to fight for a return to their homeland and to preserve their culture—to endure for more than four decades in an immigrant community. Furthermore, although second- and third-generation Cuban Americans do not necessarily share the early exiles' dreams of returning to Cuba, they tend to share their parents' and grandparents' political beliefs and the goal of a free Cuba. The

united front presented by the Cuban American community has not endured without help. Several high-profile
events in the years since the revolution have bolstered the
spirit of unity among the Cuban American community.

The Bay of Pigs

Following so shortly on the heels of the mass exile after
the revolution, the Bay of Pigs invasion was the first event
to strengthen the exiles' united front. When Fidel Castro's
new government embraced communism, President John
F. Kennedy and his advisers perceived the country as a
threat to America and began planning to overthrow Cuba's
new leader. The Central Intelligence Agency recruited and
trained Cuban exiles as counterrevolutionary forces for the
attack. On April 17, 1961, the invasion of the Bay of Pigs
was launched. It was a disaster. Under pressure from the
Soviet Union, President Kennedy withdrew his promised
air support and supplies for the forces on the ground, who
began their attack without knowing they would not be protected from the air. More than one hundred of the invaders
were killed, and the rest were taken prisoner. After more
than a year of negotiations, Castro made a deal with the
U.S. government to release 113 prisoners in exchange for
$53 million in food and medicine.

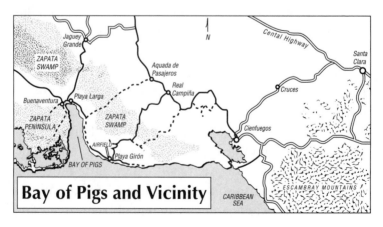

Bay of Pigs and Vicinity

The months leading up to the invasion were a time of great sacrifice and hope within the community. Most of the approximately fifteen hundred volunteers who made up the ranks of the counterrevolutionary forces—Brigade 2506—had fled Cuba when Castro took power, and they all had an intense desire to overthrow the Communist leader and reclaim their country. One of the brigade members, Jorge Marquet, describes his resolute will:

> It was a difficult decision to leave the family and run the risk of what I was going to do. Although they supported me, my wife once asked me, "How is it possible you are not thinking of your child?" I told her, "No. It is precisely because of that child and the two others I have here that I am going. I plan to return to my fatherland, and I don't want a Communist fatherland with Fidel's dictatorship."[1]

The members of Brigade 2506 were heartened by the initial support of the U.S. government, and they were certain they would be successful. They never anticipated that the United States would withdraw its support after the invasion had already begun and that the operation would be a failure. The exile community in the United States felt greatly betrayed by Kennedy, even though his administration publicly honored the brigade members and gave sincere, if vague, assertions that they would someday try again. Despite bitter feelings toward Kennedy, the exiles nurtured hope that another invasion of Cuba would be planned and carried out, and they banded together in that hope.

The brave freedom fighters of Brigade 2506 are highly honored in the Cuban American community even today. In his compilation of oral histories of the invasion, author Victor Andres Triay describes the level of respect they have attained:

> Extremely proud of their service, most are members of the Bay of Pigs Veterans Association. The group . . . has a museum in Miami's Little Havana which is frequented daily by visitors as well as retired Brigade veterans. The

men of the Brigade have always enjoyed the status of being the most distinguished and respected group among Cuban exiles. In their community, they are held in perhaps even higher regard than American veterans in the United States following World War II.[2]

To soften their position against Castro would be to dishonor their brave compatriots, so the exiles held firm in their resolve to oust the dictator. They also now had the attention of the world and were certain that it was only a matter of time before there would be another attempt to overthrow Castro. Many of the counterrevolutionary forces kept training to be ready when the call came to once again invade Cuba. The exiles' unity in this goal was strengthened and solidified despite or perhaps because of the Bay of Pigs failure. However, their hope for a second invasion was extinguished by yet another crisis in relations between the United States and Cuba: the Cuban missile crisis.

The Cuban Missile Crisis

On October 16, 1962, just eighteen months after the Bay of Pigs, the Central Intelligence Agency discovered that the Soviet Union had installed nuclear missiles in a field near San Cristobal, Cuba, and that the missiles were pointed at the United States. For the next thirteen days a tense standoff ensued between the United States and the Soviet Union. On October 22, midway through the crisis, Kennedy spoke to the nation, informing the citizens of the threat and announcing a military blockade of Cuba. As the United States braced itself for war, in Little Havana the mood alternated between elation and somberness. While most of the country perceived that the conflict was between the United States and the Soviet Union, with Cuba playing only a secondary role, most Cuban Americans saw Cuba as the focus. And some saw the crisis as an opportunity. Mark Weisenmiller describes one reaction in the

Cuban American community: "After hearing President Kennedy's announcement of a blockade, Aida Cano de Crocet, aged forty-five, had literally danced a jig in the downtown Miami restaurant where she worked. 'Wonderful, extraordinary, magnificent!' shouted de Crocet, a Miami Cuban exile; 'Fidel Castro's days are numbered.'"[3] Other exiles in Miami also praised Kennedy's speech, believing that the day was finally at hand when communism would be defeated in Cuba.

Still other exiles, however, were more cautious in their appraisal. They reasoned that if the United States went to war with the Soviet Union, and Cuba was merely the staging ground, the purpose would not be to overthrow Castro. Even worse, their friends and family on the island would be in grave peril. Churches in Little Havana remained open round the clock, offering special masses to give solace to worried Cuban Americans. They had good reason to worry. Not only was the threat of attack on the United States imminent, their beloved Cuba was also in danger of a devastating attack.

On October 29, 1962, Kennedy and Soviet leader Nikita Khrushchev reached an agreement that avoided war, but Fidel Castro was not part of the negotiations. Historian Clifford Staten describes how the agreement unfolded:

> The agreement between Kennedy and Khrushchev to remove the missiles from Cuba in exchange for a pledge by the United States not to invade the island stunned and humiliated the Cubans. The reality is that Castro and the Cubans were pawns during the missile crisis. Neither the Soviet Union nor the United States consulted with them. Castro heard about the agreement to end the crisis on the radio.[4]

Castro felt betrayed by the Soviet Union, which only bolstered his resolve to oppose all American attempts to remove him from power. Excluded from the crisis negotiations, Castro insisted on several concessions, the most painful to the exile community being Kennedy's pledge not to invade the island. The exiles' hopes for American support in toppling Castro's government seemed to be forever dashed.

Bitterly disappointed, the exile community in Little Havana came together once again. Kennedy's pledge not to mount another invasion of Cuba was a huge setback, so the exiles took another tack. Groups began forming to speak as a united voice representing the Cuban American community. Hopes for an invasion of Cuba might be gone, but the exile community would not be silent. As an organized group, they could put pressure on the U.S. government to hurt Castro in other ways, such as tightening the trade embargo. One such group, the Cuban American National Foundation, ultimately became a powerful political machine with great influence in Washington, D.C. Although the Cuban missile crisis was a devastating blow to the exiles' hope for a free Cuba, their resolve was not weakened nor was their unity shaken.

Elian Gonzalez

Other events in the years following the Bay of Pigs and the Cuban missile crisis continued to give the Cuban American community high visibility and strengthen their anti-Castro resolve. The Mariel Boat Lift of 1980, in which 125,000 Cubans were permitted to leave the island for the United States, was one event. Another was the alternate tightening and loosening of the U.S. trade embargo against Cuba. The original embargo, enacted shortly after Castro took power, was intended to punish Cuba economically in the hope that the dictator would be forced out. Subsequent presidential administrations, particularly President Bill Clinton's, eased the embargo's restrictions, and Cuban Americans were able to send money and goods as well as travel to visit friends and family in Cuba. Neither tightening nor easing the restrictions had the desired effect of removing Castro.

No single event, however, put the spotlight on Cuban Americans more than the Elian Gonzalez saga. At the center of the storm was a six-year-old boy, rescued from the sea on Thanksgiving Day in 1999 after his raft capsized and his mother drowned during an attempted escape from Cuba. After a short stay in the hospital, Elian was placed with relatives in Miami, who were adamant that the boy should remain with them and not be returned to Cuba. For five months, the Cuban American community, the U.S. government, and the entire American population debated about what should be done with Elian.

The original exiles who had fled Cuba after the revolution—and who remained anti-Castro stalwarts—fiercely believed that Elian should stay in Miami with his relatives. To return him to Cuba, they believed, would violate their principle of opposing Castro no matter what the issue. Later exile groups were not so certain. In their hearts many of them felt the young boy should be with his father, even though it meant returning him to Cuba. Mindful and respectful of the hard-line stance taken by their elders, they mostly kept quiet on the issue.

On April 22, 2000, acting on the orders of Attorney General Janet Reno, armed federal immigration agents stormed the house where Elian was staying, seized the terrified boy, and fired tear gas into an angry crowd as they left. Later that day the boy was reunited with his father in Washington, D.C., and they eventually returned to Cuba. The Cuban American community—at least those who maintained a hard-line stance against Castro—were angry and felt betrayed. And once again the exiles came together with a new resolve: to wield their political power in a way that reflected their opposition to any softened position against Fidel Castro. In the 2000 elections and again in 2004 Cuban Americans used their formidable voting power to support candidates who reflected their own vision. Even before the presidential election in 2004 they successfully pressured the administration of President George W. Bush to significantly tighten the trade embargo that had been relaxed during the Clinton administration.

The U.S. Government's Position

The U.S. government is in a quandary over what to do with Cuba, alternately sidestepping and agreeing with the sentiments of the Cuban American exiles. Abraham F. Lowenthal, a professor of international relations at the University of Southern California, analyzes the state of current policy:

> For many years, those who follow U.S. foreign policy have been resigned to the persistence of an ineffective and harmful U.S. policy toward Cuba, likely to last until Fidel Castro passes from the scene or until an administration comes to power in Washington that need not pander to the extreme anti-Castro constituency. There has been no recent sign that either contingency will materialize soon; on the contrary, they both appear to be distant possibilities.[5]

Few would argue that Cuba will not be better off when Fidel Castro is gone. Nevertheless, efforts by the United States to hasten his departure have been stunningly unsuccessful, and U.S. policy has been confusing and inconsistent. With each new U.S. president comes a different set of ideas for how to deal with Castro. Sometimes the resulting policies are in line with how the Cuban American community thinks; sometimes they are not. For the moment, the hard-line anti-Castro stance still prevails, and savvy politicians, mindful of the voting power of the multitudes of exiles in Florida, favor pressuring Castro with economic sanctions.

Today's Cuban American Community

A shift in the beliefs of the Cuban American community may be inevitable. Second- and third-generation Cuban Americans do not share the intimate connection to Cuba that their parents and grandparents have. Although they have grown up hearing about Cuba and absorbing anti-Castro sentiments, the younger generations are naturally becoming more Americanized. Many feel just as American as they do Cuban, oftentimes more. They do not have first-hand experience of the deprivations and political repression that characterize life in Cuba, and it is increasingly difficult for them to understand and sustain the hard-line stance of their elders.

As the Cuban American community changes, it is likely that their united voice, sustained for more than forty years, will change, too, as *National Review* reporter John J. Miller describes:

> It has become increasingly difficult to please huge majorities of Cuban Americans on major issues for the simple reason that views have begun to diverge. Exiles who arrived in the 1960s take a much harder line against the Castro regime than those who came here in the 1990s, according to polling by the *Miami Herald*. Most of the recent arrivals oppose the embargo—which is heresy among the older exiles.[6]

Later arrivals argue that if there was a free exchange of goods and ideas, a groundswell of protest against Castro's repressive regime would emerge in Cuba, and Castro would lose the country. Even the Cuban American National Foundation has changed its thinking. Once the political bastion of the hard-line position, the organization responded to the hysteria generated by the Elian Gonzalez episode by softening its stance, endorsing dialogue with Castro rather than confrontation.

Future generations and future exiles will continue to adopt perspectives that differ from those of the early exiles. U.S. policy will probably continue to alternate between tightening the trade embargo and favoring a more open dialogue with Castro. There is one certainty: Castro will be gone one day. How the end of his dictatorship will affect the Cuban American community in Miami, in Florida, and in the rest of the country can only be a matter of speculation.

Notes

1. Quoted in Victor Andres Triay, *The Bay of Pigs: An Oral History of Brigade 2506*. Gainesville: University Press of Florida, 2001, p. 31.
2. Triay, *The Bay of Pigs*, p. 182.
3. Mark Weisenmiller, "Florida: Front-Line State in 1962," *History Today*, October 2002, p. 38.
4. Clifford Staten, *The History of Cuba*. Westport, CT: Greenwood, 2003, p. 99.
5. Abraham F. Lowenthal, "From Bad to Worse on Cuba Policy," *San Diego Union-Tribune*, October 5, 2004, p. B7.
6. John J. Miller, "Trouble in Miami," *National Review*, October 27, 2003, p. 32.

CHAPTER 1

The Early Cuban Exiles

COMING to AMERICA

Exiles in the United States Plot to Free Cuba from Spain

Alex Antón and Roger E. Hernández

Most Latin American countries had won independence
from Spain by the 1820s, with one exception: Cuba. In the
following selection, Alex Antón and Roger E. Hernández
reveal how Cubans craved release from Spanish control but
disagreed on the path Cuba should follow. Some favored
reform and increased self-rule for Cuba while remaining
under the Spanish crown. Others favored annexation by
the United States, and still others demanded complete independence. The authors discuss the early attempts by
Cubans to carve out an identity for their country—attempts that in many cases resulted in exile to the United
States, where they continued plotting to reduce or elimi-
nate Spanish control. Antón and Hernández explore the
efforts of each faction—*reformistas, anexionistas,* and *independentistas*—showing how the Cubans began to see independence as the only option. Antón is a filmmaker and
the founding director of the Cuban Oral History Project
at St. Thomas University in Miami, Florida. Hernández is
a syndicated newspaper columnist and the author of *Cuba*
and *Cuban Immigration.*

The independence of the United States from Great Britain
was followed shortly by Latin America's own struggles for
independence from Spain. Under leaders such as the

Venezuelan Simón Bolívar and the Argentinean José de San Martín, nearly all the nations that today make up the Spanish-speaking Americas had by the 1820s defeated Spanish armies and ended Spanish rule.

In Cuba, too, there had been independence movements in the first few decades of the nineteenth century. Even though all of them were broken up by Spanish authorities, an undercurrent of resistance against colonial rule remained as Spain imposed restrictions on the rights and liberties of native-born Cubans. But Cuba was an exception to the rest of Latin America. Despite the growing sentiment in favor of independence it remained a Spanish colony when most of the other former colonies had become sovereign republics. And the principal reason may be summed up in one word: Slavery.

The brief British occupation of Havana in 1762 had brought a taste of free trade that Cubans never forgot. Fifteen years later, under pressure from Havana merchants, the Spanish colonial government finally eased restraints on foreign commerce. The restrictions were reinstated and lifted several times over the next decades but it no longer mattered. The genie was let out of the bottle and officials in a position to enrich themselves turned a blind eye to contraband during the periods of toughened regulations. As a result, Cuba experienced tremendous economic growth. Sugar exports quintupled by the mid-1780s, and a generation later Cuba was the world's largest producer.

Political Factions Emerge

The sugar boom enriched Cuba, but extracted a high price. To cut cane in the fields and work machinery in the *ingenios*—the mills that produced the precious commodity—tens of thousands of Africans were captured, brought across the Atlantic and forcibly put to work. The expanding economy demanded more slave labor, and by the beginning of the nineteenth century Cuba's black population was larger than the white. The census of 1827 found 311,051 whites, 286,942 black slaves, and 106,949 free blacks.

The influential Cuban slave owners opposed independence. They feared that a sovereign Cuba would abolish slavery and become a Haiti-style black republic, in which they would lose their fortunes and even their lives. Thus, they set Cuban independence movements decades behind those elsewhere in Latin America.

Some slave owners, fearful that slavery would be abolished even if Cuba remained under Spain, sought annexation to the United States, where they believed slavery had a future. They found support among American followers of expansion through Manifest Destiny, who prized Cuba's riches and strategic position in the Gulf. But most of all they found support among American plantation owners who overcame their reservations about annexing an island of Spanish-speaking Catholics. They understood that making Cuba a slave-owning state meant additional votes in Congress as the South tried to gain an edge in the showdown that would turn to bloodshed in the U.S. Civil War.

The different political factions that would define Cuban history for the rest of the century, on the island and in exile, were taking shape. There were *independentistas*, ready to go to war against Spain for a sovereign republic. More timid were the *reformistas*, who sought increased self-rule for Cuba but as a province under the Spanish crown. And there were *anexionistas*, themselves divided in two camps: those who sought annexation to preserve slavery, and abolitionists who wanted Cuba to join the United States because they preferred American democracy over the decrepit Spanish monarchy. All were opposed by hard-line Spaniards who wanted to rule the island not as a province of Spain but as a colony, excluding native-born Cubans from taking part in government.

Spain itself, however, was in chaos. In the decade following ouster of Napoleon from the Iberian Peninsula, Spain lost most of its empire in the Americas, and control of the government in Madrid switched four times between liberals and reactionaries. Fernando VII aligned himself with liberals when convenient only to go back to his absolutist allies as soon as they were strong enough.

A Priest Attempts Reform

It was during one of the more liberal periods that Father Félix Varela, the leading light of the first wave of Cubans who sought political refuge in the United States, came to prominence.

Varela, a Catholic priest, was an immensely popular professor of philosophy at Havana's Seminary of San Carlos, where he had taken the radical step of teaching in the vernacular—Spanish—instead of Latin, and insisted that women and men had the same right to an education. He was also the author of *Lecciones de Filosofía*, a textbook on philosophy, logic, and ethics used in universities throughout the Spanish-speaking world. Varela, a disciple wrote after his death, "taught Cubans how to think."

He would also teach Cubans to think of themselves as *Cuban*. In 1821, as a new parliament formed in Spain under a liberal constitution, enthusiastic Cubans voted for deputies to represent them at the Cortes, the Spanish congress. The three men elected, the 33-year-old Varela, Tomás Gener, and Leonardo Santos Suárez, were *reformistas*. In Madrid Varela developed detailed legislation to abolish slavery and establish self-rule for Cuba without demanding outright independence. But in 1823 this relatively democratic period in Spanish history ended with the return of absolutism. Cuba once again was made a voiceless colony rather than the semiautonomous overseas province it had become two years earlier. Parliament was dissolved and the new regime imposed the death sentence on Varela.

Varela and his fellow Cuban deputies fled Madrid and made their way to British-held Gibraltar, where they boarded the freighter *Thorndike*, bound for New York. They arrived in December 1823 during a snowstorm. Cristóbal Madan, a former student of the priest who met them at the dock, recalled later how Varela had to hold on to his arm to keep from slipping on the unfamiliar ice during the long walk to a boardinghouse on Broadway. It was the beginning of a cycle that to this day is at the heart of the Cuban-American experience: repression at home followed by exile in the United States. . . .

Annexation Gains Favor

In Cuba things progressively deteriorated. A number of separatist conspiracies had been smashed, and the Spanish government proscribed civil liberties and banned native-born Cubans from holding office or serving in the army. With 40,000 troops brought from Spain to preserve order and the Captain General in Havana ruling by martial law, the island was an armed camp. This gave renewed vigor to anticolonial sentiments, on the island and in exile.

Ironically, the most influential exiles favored annexation to the United States, not independence or even autonomy. One of the few dissenters, José Antonio Saco, raised his voice in protest. "Annexation . . . signifies the absorption of Cuba by the United States," he wrote. "I want a Cuba that is not only prosperous, learned, moral and powerful, but that Cuba be Cuban and not Anglo-American." Saco did not win many converts among fellow exiles. In the middle of the nineteenth century, *anexionistas* held sway.

The group consisted of an uneasy alliance between exiles such as [Gaspar] Betancourt Cisneros who sought the freedoms of American democracy, and representatives of rich planters who, paradoxically, wanted that democracy to protect Cuban slavery. The pro-slavery faction proved most active.

With the United States convinced of its "Manifest Destiny" after victory over Mexico, and with North and South spinning toward civil war, the notion of annexing Cuba as a slave state gained renewed strength among Americans also. Several schemes to buy the island played themselves out in 1848 and 1849, including one offer by Cuban planters to reimburse the United States $100 million if it purchased Cuba. In any case, Spain would not consider selling its most prized colony.

So it had to be tried by force. In 1848, a conspiracy was discovered in Cuba; its leader, Venezuela-born Narciso López, had risen to Field Marshal of the Spanish army during the second of Spain's Carlist civil wars. López escaped to the United States. Thus began the American saga of the most controversial figure in nineteenth-century Cuban history.

Exiles Hatch a Plot to Invade Cuba

Although the plot in which López had participated involved *independentistas*, upon arriving in the United States he began to plan for an invasion backed by *anexionistas*, Cuban as well as American. López traveled between Washington and New York, meeting with leaders of the considerable exile community that by then existed in the United States and—secretly—with Americans who might support the fight, mostly pro-slavery Southerners like the future Confederate President Jefferson Davis.

A key figure in the affair was Ambrosio José Gonzáles, who had been sent by wealthy separatists in Havana to, as he put it in an article for *The Times-Democrat* of New Orleans forty-four years later, "offer General (William Jenkins) Worth, returning home from the Mexican war, $3,000,000, wherewith to raise an expedition of 5,000 men out of the disbanded soldiers of the Mexican war and officered by the best personnel in our army, to land in Cuba in support of a patriot movement to be initiated by General Lopez with a bodyguard of Cubans and Americans."

López had to act with great delicacy: He had to keep the conspiracy secret from the anti-interventionist administration of the newly elected President Zachary Taylor; he had to entice Southerners with the idea of annexing a slave state; he had to play down the slavery issue with antislavery *anexionista* allies like Betancourt Cisneros; and he had to soft-pedal annexation with *independentistas*.

The plot progressed in fits and starts. In late 1848, Worth was named commander of federal troops in Texas and dropped out of the intrigue; the promised $3 million dried up. López persisted but in 1849 the U.S. Navy blockaded some 800 followers gathered on Round Island, off the coast of Mississippi. The same year the "*Junta Promovedora de los Intereres Políticos de Cuba*" [Committee Promoting Cuba's Political Interests], which included in its leadership López as well as the abolitionist novelist Cirillo Villaverde and even a future *independentista*, Juan Manuel Macías, began to work in Washington, New Orleans, and New York on plans for invasion. The plan was to land in Cuba, ignite a revolt, then petition for annexation.

The Cuban Flag Is Raised

The turning point came at a White House reception where Ambrosio Gonzáles was told by General John Henderson, a former Senator from Mississippi, that "if (Gonzáles) ever thought of moving in behalf of Cuba, to come to New Orleans and see him." Days later, as Gonzáles puts it, "some young gentlemen from Kentucky . . . asserted their ability and willingness to raise at their own expense and bring down to New Orleans a regiment of Kentuckians, as fine material as could be found anywhere."

López took up the offer. In New Orleans he assembled three skeleton regiments, one each from Kentucky, Mississippi, and Louisiana. So as not to arouse suspicion, López and his 600 men, with Gonzáles as second-in-command, departed separately in three vessels over twelve days. They met near Contoy Island, off Yucatan, where all boarded the steamer *Creole*. After the transfer of troops at sea, says the diary of Colonel Marion C. Taylor, a young Kentucky officer, "Gen. Lopez deputized Lt. Col. Pickett, of our regiment, to present us the flag of Cuba, as made by the Revolutionists, which was done by a few appropriate remarks, which were responded to by three cheers. It was truly an inspiring scene to behold upon the tossing billows of the ocean two vessels, upon each of which was seen the flags being presented to troops going to fight for the liberty of the oppressed of Cuba."

Landing before sunrise in Cárdenas, on the northern coast, Gonzáles recalls the men "moved in solid column toward the barracks," which they took after a firefight. The Spaniards fell back to the municipal building, which also surrendered. Then, a memorable moment in the history of Cuba: on May 19, 1850, for the first time on Cuban soil, the national flag was raised.

The invaders stayed in place. "The town was held the whole of that day. Attacks were made by the Spaniards, of infantry and cavalry from the interior, during the day, but were repulsed," Gonzáles recalled. However, Cárdenas citizens did not join López as he had expected, perhaps because there were hardly any Cubans in the nearly all-American force. When intelligence arrived that 3,000 Spanish reinforcements were on their way, López evacuated the town and under cover of night the *Creole* steamed to Key West, just beating out the pursuing Spanish cruiser *Pizarro*.

López Plots Again

Back in New Orleans, López was put on trial for violating
the Neutrality Law. The following March, after three hung
juries—the last, eleven-to-one for acquittal—charges were
dismissed. The same year authorities confiscated the
steamer *Cleopatra* in New York, again breaking up a
López plot. When President Millard Fillmore ([Zachary]
Taylor had died in office) issued arrest warrants, Gonzáles
hid in friends' plantations along coastal Georgia and South
Carolina. López went undercover in Jacksonville and Sa-
vannah; by August he was back fighting in Cuba with yet
another expedition out of New Orleans. This time he was
captured and on September 1, 1851, he was executed by
garrote. Ninety-five Americans who accompanied López
were released the following year from prison in Vigo,
Spain. When they arrived in New York that March, Cuban
refugees there collected $500 to give them "as a token of
gratitude for the noble and heroic services that these
chivalrous sons and soldiers of Liberty have rendered."

Historians have debated whether Narciso López was a
trailblazer of independence as the first patriot to lead an
organized military strike against Spanish power and fly the
Cuban flag on Cuban soil, or a renegade who nearly
wrecked Cuban nationhood by fighting to annex the island
to the United States with the expectation of preserving
slavery. If his invasion had triumphed, would he have
asked for annexation? Did he believe Cubans would go
along?

In his manifesto upon entering Cárdenas, López wrote
of "the free and independent *patria* [country]" without
mentioning annexation. In contrast, the founding decla-
ration of the Junta, which he signed, spoke of the day
Cuba could finally "take the place that corresponds to a
daughter of the Americas" and then added, echoing John
Adams nearly fifty years earlier, "before settling upon the

bosom of the great federal family." Yet it remains difficult to believe that a man of López's drive and ambition would risk his life fighting in Cuba only to meekly turn it over to the United States, whose government had even prosecuted him for his military adventures. Antonio de la Cova, professor of Latin American history at Rose-Hulman University, who specializes in this era, believes López's plan was to use American power to make himself *caudillo* [leader] of an independent Cuba.

Annexation Fades

Anexionismo survived the death of López for a few years. In New York, a new junta led by Betancourt Cisneros lobbied a willing President Franklin Pierce for annexation. But Spain indignantly turned down an offer of $120 million coupled with a threat of "direct action." Politically defeated in Washington, in 1853 the junta offered General John Quitman, a former governor of Mississippi involved with López's failed adventure, $1 million to lead a new invasion. They also arranged for a simultaneous uprising in Oriente province organized, among others, by a planter named Carlos Manuel de Céspedes.

Two years went by without Quitman taking action. Exasperated, an exile faction led by Domingo de Goicuría and José Elías Hernández took matters in its own hands. In anticipation of the uprising, they sent Francisco Estrampes and a handful of armed followers to land in Baracoa, Oriente. They were captured and garroted. The plotters who awaited disbanded. President Pierce called Quitman to the White House for a confrontation in which the Spanish minister was present. With coconspirators in Cuba routed, and with the antagonism of the Pierce administration, Quitman resigned.

A few months later the junta dissolved itself. Two proclamations in its last days, signed by the *anexionista* helmsman Betancourt Cisneros himself, enigmatically hint that, for some, *anexionismo* had been a ruse: "Annexation was the bait with which to attract the North American public," said one manifesto. Said the other, "The Revolution came to the United States to procure arms, not to assent to premature obligations of impossible incorporation."

Perhaps Betancourt Cisneros and his allies, facing the utter collapse of *anexionismo*, were simply trying to justify themselves before history by making it seem they had favored independence all along. Whatever they truly wanted, never again would *anexionista* exiles play a dominant role in Cuban politics. All their plans had ended in catastrophe. Besides, the United States began to lose interest in Cuba as Americans turned toward a more pressing domestic problem: civil war.

Spain Tightens Its Grip

With a handful of exceptions, Cubans played no major role in the American conflict. But whatever slim hopes *anexionistas* held on to ended with the abolition of slavery in America. Instead, changing circumstances in Cuba put *reformismo*, which became known as *autonomismo*, on center stage for the first time since the hopeful days a generation earlier when *reformistas* led by Félix Varela represented Cuba in the Cortes.

The early 1860s in Cuba were a time of improved relations between *criollos* [Spanish descendants] and *peninsulares*, natives of Spain. Under the liberal-minded Captain-Generals Francisco Serrano and Domingo Dulce, the colonial government opened the doors to Cubans and permitted formation of the Reformist Party, dedicated to *autonomismo*. Even a newspaper founded in New York by exile Porfirio Valiente, *El Porvenir*, circulated freely in Cuba. When Serrano went back to Spain as president of the Senate, the emboldened *autonomistas* saw in him an ally at the center of Spanish power. They asked for freer trade, for the end of the contraband slave commerce (although the importation of human beings had been outlawed by international treaty as far back as 1817, Spanish authorities and Cuban slave traders paid little attention), and for representation in the Cortes. Such demands would have earned a prison term just a few months earlier.

Madrid agreed to elections for Cuban deputies who would discuss political representation with the Spanish government. Still in exile, Betancourt Cisneros wanted nothing to do with the plan—he had no faith in Spanish promises of reform. He died in 1866, the same year the duly elected members of the *Junta de Información* [Information Committee] began arguing their cause in Madrid. His old rival José Antonio Saco was one of the deputies. But as in Varela's generation, the hopes Saco and other Cuban reformers had placed in Spanish reformers were blown away in the maelstrom of Spanish politics. Shortly after the arrival of the Cuban *autonomistas*, Serrano found himself on the losing side of a revolt. The new hard-line regime ignored the *Junta* and in 1867 sent to govern Cuba Captain-General Francisco Lersundi, who reimposed dictatorial rule. No autonomy, much less independence.

War Begins

Saco lived in Europe the remaining twelve years of his life, helplessly watching from afar as *autonomismo* grew in discredit. But one small group of exiles in New York had dissented even at the height of Serrano's popularity. Led by Juan Manuel Macías, a veteran of the Narciso López conspiracies, the "Republican Society of Cuba and Puerto Rico" published the newspaper *La Voz de América*, which called for armed revolt. The paper was regularly smuggled into the island, where it was outlawed.

These New York *independentistas* were allied with Ben-

jamin Vicuña Mackenna, a representative of the government of Chile, then at war fighting a Spanish attempt to re-
gain its former colony. In 1866, Chilean leaders, hoping to
open a second front in the Caribbean, authorized Mackenna
to tell Macías that Chile would aid a revolution if Cubans
took the first step. The old dream of help from Latin America seemed about to come true. But Macías's followers could
not manage to raise more than a few hundred dollars. Chile
lost interest after Spanish ships withdrew from its ports on
the Pacific.

It did not matter. With *anexionismo* dead for a decade,
autonomismo in tatters after Governor Lersundi's reactionary policies, and abolition made inevitable by Lincoln's
Emancipation Proclamation, Cubans began to see independence as the only option. The feeling was particularly strong
among the small planters of Oriente in eastern Cuba, who
were isolated from the politics of Havana and, with smaller
landholdings and fewer slaves than the sugar barons in the
west, had less to lose. In Spain the liberal Serrano regained
power, but it was too late to stop the avalanche.

On October 10, 1868, Carlos Manuel de Céspedes freed
his 37 slaves at La Demajagua, a small sugar plantation near
the town of Yara, and rose in arms with little more than 100
men. A month later, Céspedes held the large towns of
Bayamo and Holguín with an army of 12,000. The Ten
Years War in Cuba had begun.

Cuban Exiles Transform Florida

Alejandro Portes and Alex Stepick

Even before Cuba gained independence in 1898, Florida in general, and Miami in particular, was a haven for Cuban exiles. This tradition continued through the Spanish-American War and the political regimes that followed. In the following selection, authors Alejandro Portes and Alex Stepick trace the repeating pattern of regime change followed by new waves of exiles to Florida during the late 1800s and the early 1900s. The authors also explore how Miami evolved into a political base for exiles plotting to overthrow whichever leader happened to be in power at the time. Portes is a professor of sociology at Princeton University in New Jersey and the author of *Latin Journey: Cuban and Mexican Immigrants in the United States.* Stepick is the director of the Immigration and Ethnicity Institute, professor of sociology and anthropology at Florida International University in Miami, and the author of *This Land Is Our Land: Immigrants and Power in Miami.*

Tucked among the royal palms and frangipani of South Street in Key West, the southernmost urban way in the United States, is the John Dewey House. The bungalow was the winter home of the famous American philosopher, who found in this community and its weather a balmy respite from the rigors of the north. It is a white wooden structure built in a style familiar throughout the Caribbean; it looks south toward Cuba.

Less than two blocks away, as one turns north onto Duval Street, El Balcón de Martí, the second-story balcony from which the Cuban revolutionary José Martí addressed throngs of exiled cigar workers commands the sidewalk. The humble monetary contributions of those workers, plus similar collections in Tampa and Jacksonville, armed a series of expeditions against the Spanish colonial regime in the island during the 1890s. Today the building graced by El Balcón houses an inn and a fancy restaurant.

One block north along Duval is the San Carlos Club, a structure reminiscent of the architecture of old Havana but actually built in the 1920s to replace a nineteenth-century gathering place of Cuban revolutionaries. The new San Carlos was dedicated on October 10, 1924, the anniversary of the beginning of the first Cuban war of independence. The building's founding stone was brought from *La Demajagua*, the sugar mill where that rebellion started. . . .

Independence Is Bittersweet

Miami in the late 1890s was as yet too insignificant to serve as a base for conspiracies and was thus spared the revolutionary fever. . . .

The Spanish-American War was the first major event to unite the destinies of the young Florida city and the island colony. Shortly after the hostilities began, the U.S. Army moved troops to Camp Miami in preparation for invading the island. As it turned out, no invasion took place because the Spanish resistance crumbled quickly; instead the idle troops amused themselves by harassing the inhabitants of Colored Town. It would not be the last time that affairs in Cuba would end up with the victimization of Blacks in Miami.

The defeat of Spain was a bittersweet victory for the Cubans. As the exile colonies of Tampa and Key West began to empty out, the returning revolutionaries carried to the island ambivalent feelings toward the country that had given them refuge. True, the American intervention had brought a bloody war to a swift end, but the favor had come at a cost: Cuba was now a political protectorate. American generals governed the island from 1898 to 1902, and when they finally left, the new republic found that it was anything but fully independent. Senator Orville H. Platt proposed, and the U.S. Congress approved, an amendment to the Cuban constitution giving Washington the right to intervene in the country's internal affairs. Under the Platt Amendment, the American ambassador became in point of fact the colonial overseer of Cuba.

With such political assurances in place, U.S. capital started pouring into the island. The pattern of investment was not too different from that taking place in Florida at the same time: money went into agriculture, primarily sugar cane, and tourist ventures. In 1902, the most plausible future for the nascent republic was as a southern extension of Florida, formally independent but subject to the economic and cultural hegemony of the north. Had this occurred, the remarkable counterpoint of Yankee developers and Cuban revolutionaries that was so apparent in South Florida during the 1890s would not have repeated itself. Instead the homogenizing logic of capital, bent on extracting profit from warmer weather and fertile land on both sides of the Straits of Florida, would have prevailed.

That things did not turn out that way is a consequence primarily of the kind of country Cuba was. . . .

Exiles Use Florida as a Political Base

Although weaker economically, Cuba was a very different place from the semivacant peninsula. Instead of becoming its appendage, Cuba gradually converted Florida into her own political backstage, where the dramas, and sometimes comedies, of exile were regularly enacted. The counterpoint of the late 1890s was hence repeated, but each time with a different cast of characters and a slight alteration of place. Now, as Miami continued to develop along the lines envisioned by its founders, the upheavals of Cuban politics regularly deposited a new wave of exiles on its shores.

For many years, the resort-bound vacationers and political conspirators coexisted in the city with the same mutual indifference they had exhibited in Key West during the Spanish-American War. Polly Redford's history of Miami, which ends before the Cuban Revolution, contains only two references to Cubans, both as hired help in Miami Beach hotels. In turn, Hugh Thomas's voluminous history of Cuba does not have a single index entry for Miami, even though much political maneuvering went on there in the twentieth century. For Miami hotel owners and developers, Cubans represented little more than an occasional source of low-wage labor. For the exiles, the city was but a rear base for organizing offensives against the government in Havana.

Several factors contributed to this casual attitude of Cubans toward a city that was, after all, in a different country. Weather and geography played a part, no doubt, but so did the built environment. Old Key West had been built by Cubans, and its architecture naturally reflected styles familiar in the island. Miami was built by Yankee developers, but their blueprints were also dominated by Andalusian and Mediterranean themes. Up and down the beach, wrought iron, red tile, and villas with Spanish names abounded. An architecture designed to attract tourists came to provide, unwittingly, a receptive setting for former Spanish colonials.

Machado's Government Triggers More Exiles

When General Gerardo Machado, democratically elected president of Cuba, decided to change the constitution in the late 1920s so that he could stay indefinitely in power, he triggered a new flow of exiles going to both Miami and New York. The Platt Amendment, still in force, enabled the U.S. ambassadors to Cuba to play a key role in the ensuing struggle. American economic interests in the island, moreover, supported the dictator, just as they had supported the colonial regime during the war of independence. "Indeed," Thomas observes, "it was all too easy for both government and opposition to slip into the roles of Spaniards and Nationalists—with the U.S. playing a similar if more ambiguous role than in the 1890s: its home territory acting as a base for rebels, its citizens in Cuba being a support for the Cuban government, both helping to provide specific financial assistance."

The American ambassador, Sumner Welles, was at first friendly toward Machado, but soon the increasing violence and political instability in Cuba persuaded him that the general had to go. Thus, through Welles's efforts, the first Cuban dictatorship came to an end: on August 12, 1933, Machado flew to Nassau with a few friends—some still in their pajamas—and seven bags of gold. Many of his closest supporters ended up in Miami, where Machado was eventually buried. His tomb is in the Woodlawn Cemetery, today in the heart of Little Havana.

The intense participation of the American ambassador in the events of 1933, as well as the comings and goings between Washington and Havana under the Platt Amendment, gave Cubans an object lesson in the politics of empire. The unfortunate status of being a semicolony had the unintended effect of giving the islanders a thorough apprenticeship in the political ways of the north. The Cuban upper class learned henceforth to monitor the government in Washington as carefully as they did their own in Havana.

In Miami, those August days of 1933 had witnessed the departure of exultant revolutionaries, their places taken by crestfallen incoming *machadistas*. The city, however, was in no mood to pay much attention to this change of the guard: it was in big trouble. The land boom of the nineteen twenties had turned into a complete bust, and the population had declined by more than half in less than ten years. The Royal Palm Hotel was boarded up, and many other businesses had closed. With no paying jobs anywhere, locals rediscovered the natural bounty of the tropics, nearly forgotten since the arrival of [Henry] Flagler's railroad. Avocadoes, mangoes, and guavas were still plentiful in Miami backyards, and fish still swam in great numbers in the bay; the subsistence that they provided came to substitute for store-bought provisions. As the despondent Machado exiles made their appearance, they found a city where a good part of the economy had reverted to what it had been half a century earlier, replacing that run on tourist dollars and rampant land speculation.

Castro Emerges

On a sunny day twenty-three years later, the authorities of Daytona Beach gathered to honor a famous local resident. The man in question, General Fulgencio Batista y Zaldívar, had left Daytona a few years earlier to organize opposition to the democratically elected president of Cuba, Carlos Prío y Socarrás. On March 10, 1952, Batista engineered a military coup that sent Prío packing to Mexico and eventually to Miami. The new regime was very favorably disposed to Americans, be they legitimate businessmen or gambling racketeers, and the sugar-led prosperity of the island insured happy returns to all. Accordingly, the Daytona city fathers saw nothing wrong in proclaiming March 24, 1956, "Batista Day" in honor of the new Cuban dictator, in a ceremony held only a few hundred miles away from Miami, where the deposed legitimate president sulked in impotence.

Prío was down but not out. He now dedicated all his en-

ergies and his considerable personal fortune to the overthrow of Batista. And although Prío was not up to leading
an expedition himself, he supported almost anyone who
did. First the Luzerne Hotel in Miami Beach and then
Prío's own Casa Reposada in South Miami became hubs of
conspiracy where politicians and adventurers of all stripes
came to avail themselves of the former president's largesse.
Miami once again became the center of opposition to the
regime in Havana.

It was thus to Miami that, in late 1955, a young exile
came who could boast of having led the only major armed
attack on Batista's dictatorship. The attack failed, and
many of the participants were killed, but Fidel Castro survived and was amnestied two years later. Although Castro
had been an active political opponent of former President
Prío, all was forgotten now in the two men's common
struggle against the Batista dictatorship. From Miami,
therefore, Fidel was able to take back to his headquarters
in Mexico a hefty financial contribution and the promise
of more to come. One year later, Fidel and his band of revolutionaries embarked on the fifty-eight-foot yacht
Granma, bought with $15,000 of Prío's money, and
landed in Oriente Province, Cuba, on December 2, 1956.

From that day until the overthrow of Batista in 1959,
the center of revolutionary action shifted to the Sierra
Maestra Mountains, where the rebels had established their
headquarters. Miami became a support base. Thenceforth
a tacit struggle broke out between Castro supporters, whose
mission was to send arms and supplies to the rebels, and the
rest of the anti-Batista factions, who felt increasingly up-
staged. Prío's plan had succeeded only too well in creating
an armed challenge to the dictatorship, but in the process
the deposed president had lost control of the situation.

An attempt to bring the revolution back into the hands
of those who were paying for it was made in Miami in the

early winter of 1957. At a meeting attended by representatives of Castro's Twenty-sixth of July Movement, Prío's
Autentico party, and other exile factions, a Council of National Liberation was established, with Prío's former prime
minister, Manuel Antonio de Varona, named head. The
council immediately issued a manifesto designed to reas-
sure both Washington and the Cuban elite about the revolution's procapitalist leanings. Prío, who helped organize
the meeting and who financed most of the groups present,
emerged as the clear winner.

There was one hitch, however, and that was that Fidel
Castro had never been consulted. He learned about the "Miami Pact" in the *New York Times* and immediately de-
nounced it. His protest letter to the council exemplifies the
language he would use to silence all opposition after his arrival in power: "For those who are fighting against an army
incomparably greater in number and arms, with no support
for a whole year apart from the dignity with which we are
fighting . . . bitterly forgotten by fellow countrymen who,
in spite of being well provided for, have systematically . . .
denied us their help, the Miami Pact was an outrage."

With the withdrawal of Castro's Twenty-sixth of July
Movement and later of other forces, the council disinte-
grated. The exile community in Miami was thereafter torn
in a double struggle: against Batista and between the increasingly dominant *fidelistas* and other revolutionary
groups. Prío helped organize and finance several subsequent expeditions, aimed at balancing the increasing hegemony of the Sierra Maestra rebels. But it was too late. Fidel Castro had captured both the imagination of Cubans
and the fancy of the U.S. press, and when Batista finally
fled on December 31, 1958, power fell right into the hands
of the Sierra Maestra leader. Other revolutionary groups
were compelled to fall into line or were eliminated.

In the wake of Fidel's triumph, many Miami Cubans returned to their homeland. Like the returning exiles of 1895, they harbored decidedly mixed feelings about the country left behind. True, the United States had given them refuge, and influential American voices had supported their cause, but the U.S. government had also waited until the last minute to reverse its active support of Batista. Like the Daytona Beach city council, State Department officials put North American economic concerns first and human rights and democracy in Cuba a definitive second. . . .

As for ex-president Prío, the early patron of Castro's rebel movement, he was courted at first by the new regime, which sent him on a series of diplomatic sorties abroad. Deprived of any real power and confronted with a radicalizing revolution, though, he sought asylum during one such trip to Brazil. A few days later, he was back in Miami. Years later, his fortune and influence gone, he committed suicide at his home in Coral Gables. Like Gerardo Machado, he is buried in the Woodlawn Cemetery, in the middle of Little Havana.

Cuban American Life During the 1950s

James S. Olson and Judith E. Olson

During the 1950s, when travel between Cuba and the United States was unrestricted, the lure of economic prosperity convinced tens of thousands of Cubans to leave their homeland. Many realized their dreams, but there was a price to be paid. In this selection, authors James S. and Judith E. Olson describe the racial, economic, religious, and political differences that often led to discrimination and difficult working conditions for Cuban Americans. The authors also explain how differences arose within the Cuban American community itself, creating internal strife among the immigrants. James Olson is a professor of history at Sam Houston State University in Texas. Judith Olson is the former director of the Learning Assistance Center and teacher of bilingual education, also at Sam Houston University.

Like every other ethnic community in the United States, Cuban America was divided by a series of profound racial, economic, religious, and political differences. Political and social life in the Cuban-American community revolved around a kaleidoscope of rich and poor, black and white, Catholic and Protestant, and liberal, conservative, and radical perspectives. The Cuban working classes in the United States were struggling for economic survival. Cigar manufacturers had first moved to the United States in the 1870s to avoid political and social instability on the island and se-

James S. Olson and Judith E. Olson, *Cuban Americans: From Trauma to Triumph*. New York: Twayne Publishers, 1995. Copyright © 1995 by James S. Olson and Judith E. Olson. All rights reserved. Reproduced by permission of the Gale Group.

cure a good supply of cheap labor. Depending on where the political atmosphere was most propitious for low wages and labor exploitation, cigar manufacturers would shift economic assets and investment capital back and forth. It was clear to them as well as to the workers that Key West, Tampa, and Havana were all within a single economic orbit. Workers sympathized with one another's problems and supported one another's strikes. Unless they could establish a united front, they stood no chance of improving their economic circumstances. Cuban workers in Florida and Cuba believed in labor organization, labor legislation, and a liberal social and economic agenda. They were highly politicized and acutely aware of their own economic predicament. Their managerial and corporate counterparts in Cuba and the United States, not surprisingly, were conservative and anti-union.

The Cuban workers in the United States found themselves in difficult political and social circumstances, primarily because Florida was part of the deep South. Southern tobacco, cotton, and sugar planters had always been notoriously anti-union; the last thing they wanted was the large-scale organization of poor blacks and whites in the fields and mills. In fact, many Florida whites were especially anti-Cuban because of the popularity radical political theories had traditionally had among Cuban-American workers. Although there were profound differences in philosophy between Karl Marx and [independence hero] José Martí, southerners were not aware of them. Most southerners viewed the Cuban workers as a kind of radical vanguard, and by the 1950s, during the Red Scare, more than a few southern politicians voiced concern about the possibility of Communist cells in South Florida.

Immigrants Face Racism

Many Cuban-American workers also faced the dilemma of being black in the American South. Most of the workers were Afro-Cubans, and most white southerners had no love lost for black people, whether they spoke Spanish or English. The fact that the Afro-Cubans were also highly politicized only made them appear more threatening. During the labor strikes of the 1930s and 1950s, especially when integration fears were blossoming after the Supreme Court's *Brown v. Board of Education of Topeka, Kansas*, decision in 1954, the Ku Klux Klan targeted what it called the "Cuban niggers" for a reign of terror. With the tacit and sometimes enthusiastic support of local law-enforcement agencies, the Klan joined forces with manufacturers to crush strikes, intimidate workers, and beat up and kill union organizers. The Klan's ubiquitous burning crosses often lit up the night in the Afro-Cuban neighborhoods. At the same time, the FBI and the CIA launched clandestine investigations of those communities, hoping to turn up secret Communist groups planning anti-American activities.

South Florida was not much more hospitable for poor Cuban whites. During the nineteenth and early twentieth centuries, immigrants to the United States did not normally settle in the South. Its reputation for racism and ethnocentrism kept many immigrants away, as did its retarded economy and system of labor exploitation. The vast majority of southern whites in the 1950s were descendents of those English and Scots-Irish immigrants who had arrived in the United States during the eighteenth and nineteenth century. Not surprisingly, southern whites were not very accustomed to immigrants or ethnic diversity. Also, because of the outcome of the Civil War, they often had an extremely negative, hostile attitude about racial and ethnic differences. For them, moral virtue in any decent society was concentrated in the white community. Far more so than in the great immigrant cities of the Northeast, native southern whites had no sense of cultural pluralism. And the only real enduring diversity in southern ethnic life—the division between whites and blacks—had been a source of strain and violence, not strength. Afro-Cubans were forced to live in separate neighborhoods, and Afro-Cuban children were segregated into separate schools with southern black children. The children of Cuban whites were forbidden to speak Spanish in the public schools, even during lunch and recess. Drop-out rates were very high, and the resulting poverty severe. Job discrimination and such phrases as "Cubans need not apply" became all too common.

Religious Discrimination Emerges

Religion was also a distinguishing feature of the Cuban working class in Florida. Southern white culture was dominated by Protestantism—a fundamental Protestantism that was imbued with unusual passion and that played a central role in the cultural identity of the region. During the nineteenth century the major Protestant denominations of the South—Baptists, Presbyterians, Methodists, and Episcopalians—had split with their northern brethren over the slavery issue. The notion of being a white Baptist or a white Presbyterian or a Pentecostal acquired a great deal of power. During the twentieth century, as biblical criticism and modern scholarship progressed in northern universities, southerners became more and more committed to a strict interpretation of their "old time religion." They interpreted the Bible literally, rejected outright any belief in evolution, and maintained a powerful evangelical point of view.

They were also intensely anti-Catholic. To southern Protestants, Roman Catholicism represented an alien religion inherently different from the spirit of American institutions. For Catholics, spiritual sovereignty was contained in the priesthood authority that emanated from the pope in Rome to bishops and then to parish priests and finally to individual worshipers. That seemed antidemocratic to most white southerners, who believed in congregational autonomy and in the idea that no living human being controlled the gates of heaven. From the 1920s into the 1950s southern Protestants felt they detected all kinds of Roman Catholic plots and conspiracies to take over America; they were especially concerned about the large-scale Roman Catholic immigration to the United States from Ireland, eastern and southern Europe, and Latin America. During the twentieth century, the Ku Klux Klan added Catholics and Jews to its list of enemies of the United States. The Klan also spread out of the South into the urban centers of the North where resentment about immigration was increasing.

So in addition to being African and Hispanic in background as well as highly politicized in their backgrounds, the working-class Cubans in Florida were also heavily Roman Catholic, which made them even more suspect as far as southern Protestants were concerned. The irony, of course; was that Cubans were the least religious, at least in terms of formal Catholicism, of any Roman Catholic group in the United States. . . .

Immigrants Find Prosperity

A substantial number of middle-class Cubans and their descendents had moved to the United States during the twentieth century purely for economic reasons and found prosperity. Because the economy of Cuba was so heavily vested in large-scale commercial agriculture—coffee, sugar, and tobacco—there was little room for a middle class. Cuban society was divided by a huge lower class, a tiny upper class, and a middle class that was not much larger. There were not enough rich people to consume the services of large numbers of middle-class professionals, nor were there enough poor people who could afford them. Consequently, the United States became the beneficiary during the twentieth century of a steady flow of highly educated teachers, lawyers, accountants, physicians, dentists, engineers, librarians, professors, pharmacists, journalists, nurses, technologists, architects, and scientists. They simply could not make a living in Cuba. There was also a small group of wealthy Cuban-American families involved in the cigar-manufacturing business. The Vicente Martínez Ybor family, for example, had relocated their cigar factories to Florida in the late nineteenth century and there acted like "Robber Barons," with attitudes not unlike those of [industrialist] Andrew Carnegie or [railroad magnate] George Pullman. In fact, they had also moved their operations from Key West to what became known as Ybor City outside of Tampa to escape organized labor. Ybor City was originally a company town where the lives of workers were completely controlled by management. Other prominent cigar-manufacturing families, such as the Gatos and the Piños, created similar barrios where organized labor was not permitted. Although that company-town mentality had disappeared by the 1950s, there were nevertheless several thousand Cuban Americans whose wealth had come from the cigar sweatshops of the late nineteenth and early twentieth centuries.

Finally, on both sides of the Straits of Florida, there were tens of thousands of Cubans whose economic livelihood depended on the continuation of the status quo. Unlike the Cuban-American working classes, who were often radical in their politics, mixed in their racial background, and Catholic-Santería in their religion, the more well-to-do Cuban Americans were politically conservative, white, and often Protestant. A great economic, social, and political chasm divided the two groups, and it was not unlike some of the class divisions on the island that would soon bring about another revolution.

It was not surprising, given the close economic ties between the Cuban elite and the United States, that they were almost as much American as they were Cuban, sharing a great deal with upper-class Cuban Americans. The devastation of the Ten Years' War convinced thousands of well-to-do Cubans that their investment capital was safer in American banks than in Cuba. Large numbers of Cubans increased their dollar investments as a way of protecting themselves economically against political instability in Cuba. Each time Cuban politics erupted in civil war or revolution, the flow of capital to the United States increased and the linkages between upper-class groups in Cuba and the United States grew stronger.

The Cuban elite developed an even more unique strategy for protecting themselves against instability on the island. Beginning late in the nineteenth century, increasing numbers of well-to-do Cubans sought and achieved U.S. citizenship. Thousands of rich Cubans became naturalized American citizens, which then allowed them to appeal for U.S. protection of their property. When local disputes caused property damage, these "Cuban Americans" could demand reparations and expect U.S. support for their demands. And because there were so many well-to-do Americans living in Cuba and managing corporate assets there, a good deal of intermarriage occurred between the children of the two elites over the years. Since the child of a U.S. citizen was automatically an American citizen or was eligible to apply for it, there were thousands of "Cuban Americans" on the island who had never really lived in the United States for any extended period. Like their counterparts in the United States, they had only the most conservative expectations of a Cuban government.

But money was not the only thing upper-class *criollos* [Spanish descendents] were sending to the United States. Because school facilities were so lacking on the island, the Cuban elite usually sent their children to the United States for an education. An American education was also an entré for economic success on the island. Many well-to-do Cuban children attended private primary schools, secondary schools, and colleges in the United States, spending their entire childhood and adolescence away from home, becoming more American in outlook than Cuban. Many of them married school sweethearts and took out American citizenship. They even adopted English as their primary language, using Spanish only when they returned home to Cuba for visits.

With their money and their children often living in the United States, they found themselves frequent travelers in America. By the 1940s and early 1950s the regular steamship and ferry traffic between several American ports and Havana was augmented by regular air service between Havana and New York City, Chicago, Philadelphia, Baltimore, New Orleans, and Miami. Wealthy Cubans traveled to the United States to visit their children, relatives, and corporate clients, as well as to hit the most popular vacation spots. They came to the United States to secure sophisticated medical treatment. Finally, and most often, they came to America to shop. That process too had a tremendous effect on Cuban society because the Cuban elite began to use an American frame of reference in judging economic success. That they were well off compared to Latin American standards was no longer enough; they also wanted to be well off by North American standards.

Creation of the Golden Exiles

In addition to adopting American consumer culture, many Cubans converted to Protestantism. After the Spanish-American War a variety of Protestant denominations began evangelizing crusades in Cuba, dividing up the island into spheres of influence. Baptist, Methodist, Congregationalist, Lutheran, Presbyterian, and Quaker ministers and missionaries fanned out across the island trying to win converts. They encountered a great deal of success, some because there were religiously devout people looking for an alternative to Catholicism, and others simply because conversion to Protestantism seemed to be socially and economically prudent given the American domination of the island. By the 1950s there were more than 400,000 Protestants in Cuba, and the number of Protestant ministers and chapels outnumbered the number of Catholic priests and churches. Although Catholics still far outnumbered Protestants on the island, Protestants probably outnumbered Catholics on Sunday morning in terms of church attendance throughout the island.

What evolved over the course of the twentieth century was the creation of an upper class in Cuba that had been educated in American schools and was often bilingual in English and Spanish, Protestant or nominal Roman Catholic in religion, conservative in political and economic orientation, intimately linked with the American corporate world by investment or employment, and familiar with or faithful to the products of the American consumer culture and the icons of American popular culture. There are literally thousands of examples of this profile in the Cuban upper class. Tomás Estrada Palma, the man the United States designated as the first president of an independent Cuba in 1902, was a naturalized U.S. citizen, a Quaker, and a fluent speaker of English. Mario Menocal, who served as president of Cuba from 1912 to 1920, had a degree from Cornell University and had been a longtime employee of the Cuban-American Sugar Company. Demetrio Castillo Duany, who became governor of Oriente Province, was a naturalized American citizen who had lived in New York City and studied at the New York School of Commerce. Perfecto Lacosta, longtime mayor of Havana, had a degree from the University of Pennsylvania. With their North

American friends, they had joined the yacht, jockey, Rotary, Lions, Kiwanis, and Optimists clubs; they joined the chambers of commerce, Masonic Lodges, country clubs, American Legion, Daughters of the American Revolution, women's clubs, tennis clubs, athletic clubs, Little League, United Spanish War Veterans, YMCA, YWCA, Women's Christian Temperance Union, and a host of other recreational and civic organizations. If "Little Havanas" existed in some of the cities of South Florida, there were "Little Americas" in several cities of the north coast of Cuba, and in most cases certain Cubans were invited to join.

Unlike any other group of ethnic Americans in the 1950s, or throughout U.S. history for that matter, the Cuban-American community existed in the new country as well as in the old. There were nearly 125,000 people of Cuban descent living in the United States, but there were thousands more in Cuba whose cultural, economic, and political ties to America were extremely tight. There were nearly 6 million people living in Cuba in the mid-1950s. In addition to the 10,000 or 15,000 people who were truly upper class, there were another 600,000 Cubans who worked as middle-class professionals, corporate managers, office workers, and marketing personnel, and most of them directly depended on the links between the Cuban and North American economies. When Fidel Castro marched triumphantly into Havana in 1959, there was a strong anti-American, class dimension to the revolution. The lives of those hundreds of thousands of white, English-speaking, Protestant, well-to-do, conservative Cubans were vulnerable to dramatic change. They would become the "Golden Exiles" to the United States.

The "Golden Exiles" Find Refuge in America

Miguel Gonzalez-Pando

When Fidel Castro took power in 1959, thousands of middle- and upper-class Cubans fled to Florida, fearing persecution because their elite status did not fit with the philosophy of the revolution. These immigrants came to be known as the "Golden Exiles" because, for the most part, they were well-to-do, highly educated professionals. As Miguel Gonzalez-Pando reveals in the following selection, their life in the United States was much different from the comfortable existence they had known in Cuba. The author shows how these exiles juggled the need to survive with the desire to overthrow Castro and return to their homeland. Gonzalez-Pando is the founder of the Cuban Living History Project at Florida International University.

Cubans began their [Fidel] Castro-era emigration the moment General Fulgencio Batista fled the island on New Year's morning of 1959 and a provisional revolutionary government took over the reins of the politically troubled nation. The first exiles were hundreds of Batista's closest collaborators who feared reprisals from the regime that had ousted them. Soon after, they were joined in the United States by a massive exodus that originated within the nation's business establishment and professional class but quickly enough included early defectors from Castro's own ranks as well. That initial exodus, therefore, embraced

Miguel Gonzalez-Pando, *The Cuban Americans*. Westport, CT: Greenwood Press, 1998. Copyright © 1998 by Miguel Gonzalez-Pando. All rights reserved. Reproduced by permission of the publisher.

three distinct exile "vintages," the largest of which was the island's nonpolitical elite.

The upper and middle classes were disproportionately represented in that initial wave. Because of political circumstances, the emigrés were mostly destitute upon arrival, but many of them were familiar with the United States, having often visited it for business or pleasure before the revolution. Some also had old schoolmates, friends, and business contacts throughout the nation. In addition, because Cuban culture was highly Americanized, the members of this particular vintage were not complete strangers to America's way of life: To them, the United States was not terra incognita. Precisely because of their familiarity with the United States, they "were the least given to believe that the American government would permit the consolidation of a socialist regime in the island."

> These were people who had it all in Cuba. They were living comfortable lives, they were professionals, they were well-adjusted, and they gave it all up because they wanted their children to live in an environment of freedom. They wanted to free Cuba; they came to this country with the idea that this was the place from where to organize the struggle for Cuba's freedom, where their children could grow and develop their full potential—something they couldn't do in Cuba. (Author's interview with attorney Rafael Peñalver)

The demographic profile of the exiles who arrived between 1959 and 1962 confirms other characteristics associated with their high socioeconomic status in prerevolutionary Cuba. Most may have left empty handed but not without human capital. Their educational and professional backgrounds, in fact, placed them near the top echelons of society—in Cuba and in America as well. This wave constituted the island's "cream of the crop"—those who had studied English at Havana's private schools or had learned it at American summer camps, high schools, and colleges. They were also older than most immigrants; hence, their cultural identity was rather defined by the time they left their homeland, a crucial factor in understanding how this group was able to resist becoming acculturated in America.

The role that their identity as exiles has played on their American dynamics defies quantification; so do other defining traits displayed by this initial wave, such as pride, enterprising drive, adaptability, and a host of other psychosocial aspects that served them well in their new environment. Neither can the cultural "baggage" they brought be accurately measured by statistics. The same is true of their political idiosyncrasies. Perhaps there is something unique in the mind-set of all exiles that acts as a special incentive to do well. In any event, the initial wave of Cuban emigrés had it in abundance. They were also heirs to an enterprising tradition honed by centuries of commercial contact with the outside world, which may account for the self-confident attitude generally found among the winners—and these Cubans were definitely not wanting in the determination to succeed.

The Anti-Castro Struggle Among Early Exiles

Upon their arrival in the United States, the initial wave was driven by one all-consuming objective: to return to Cuba after toppling Castro's revolutionary government. They expected that, with the support of their powerful American ally, such an objective would be accomplished within a short period of time. This expectation was not the result of wishful thinking; rather, it was a most natural assumption. Indeed, given the geopolitical interest Americans had historically shown in its Cuban neighbors, it seemed inconceivable that a Communist regime would be allowed to take hold within the U.S. sphere of influence.

Those first exiles reasoned that Castro did not stand a

chance of remaining in power for long. Truly, the odds against the survival of the revolutionary regime seemed formidable. By the summer of 1960, guerilla groups linked to an incipient underground network had already surfaced in the Cuban mountains ("armed bandits," Castro called them). More ominously, the U.S. government had begun to recruit and train exiles for paramilitary actions against Castro. Such internal and external threats, the exiles inferred, could not be effectively countered by the nascent regime.

By early 1961, right after the inauguration of President [John F.] Kennedy, the emigrés' confidence in the liberation of their homeland reached a feverish pitch, as scores of Cuban exiles were being recruited by the Central Intelligence Agency (CIA) and sent to training bases in Guatemala and other secret locations. This was supposed to be a covert operation, but pictures of the training camps were prominently displayed in the weekly tabloids (*periodiquitos*) published in the United States by exiles as well as in *The New York Times*. Despite President Kennedy's repeated denials, everyone was well aware that a U.S.-sponsored invasion of the island would soon be launched. That prospect, certainly, was viewed as the coup de grâce for the fledgling revolutionary government.

The invasion fever sweeping the Cuban exile community became obsessive. A coalition of anti-Castro groups had been brought together under the auspices of "The Company"—the term used by the personnel of the CIA. The new umbrella organization, Consejo Revolucionario Cubano (Cuban Revolutionary Council), came under the political and military control of the CIA, making the exiles nothing more than willing instruments of the United States. Although the relinquishing of total authority to the CIA caused some friction among exile leaders, they were persuaded that this was an "unavoidable cost." The plans for the invasion continued at full speed.

The Need for Survival

Although their attention remained focused on the liberation of Cuba, the exiles still needed to find the means to survive during what they assumed would be a temporary stay in America. Since many did not speak fluent English, finding that first job represented a formidable challenge; an ever-expanding pool of exiles competed for limited local jobs. South Florida was clearly a buyers' market.

> It was Halloween night when I arrived in Miami with my wife and my one-year-old son. I saw the kids "trick-or-treating" and only $40 in my pocket. . . . We found a room to live in a house with an old lady—$5 a week was our room, one bed, all three of us slept in the one bed. But at last we were in the land of freedom and democracy and opportunity. (Author's interview with banker Carlos Arboleya)

For the exiles in those days, making ends meet meant accepting the first job that was offered. Since South Florida's strong unions maintained firm restrictions against the newcomers, Cubans were forced to take any jobs, even those traditionally held by Miami's African Americans. Former Cuban entrepreneurs and professionals parked cars, washed dishes, drove taxis, waited on tables, delivered newspapers, and performed a variety of menial tasks for which they were undoubtedly overqualified. Unlicensed Cuban doctors and dentists, ever so careful not to be discovered by the authorities, saw patients in their own homes. Housewives who had never held a job in Cuba found employment as waitresses, maids, seamstresses, factory workers, and vegetable pickers in the fields. Thousands of exiles were able to go on the generous payroll of the CIA, which during the Survival Stage may have been one of Dade County's larger employers.

The challenge of survival was met with a strong sense of solidarity. In South Florida, where the bulk of the emigrés waited for Castro's overthrow, those who arrived earlier tried to ease the shock of the newly arrived by offering them advice on how to obtain a social security card, to enroll their children in school, to look for housing, and to enlist in the federally funded Cuban Refugee Program, where they could get free medical attention and bags of groceries. The few fortunate enough to afford a car drove their Cuban neighbors to work, to the doctor, and to supermarkets. Typically, they helped each other find jobs, and once hired, they recommended friends and relatives to their employers.

> Grass roots organization started practically in the beginning in the 60s. People didn't lose track of where they came from or their families and friends, and that facilitated the creation of an economic and social network that was going to contribute greatly to the Cuban success. (Author's interview with anthropologist Mercedes Sandoval)

Whether in the South Florida area or in other American cities, Cubans in those days seldom made a move outside their closely knit circle of family and lifelong acquaintances. The spirit of community that characterized the Survival Stage was to prevail until today, as each new wave went through a similar process upon arriving in America. Survival, indeed, became the shared rite of passage into exile.

Settling in South Florida

Given their expectations for a quick return to their homeland, the initial exodus settled primarily in and around Miami. That was understandable. Throughout the island's brief history as an independent nation, South Florida's proximity to Cuba had made it the haven of choice whenever political troubles forced Cubans into exile. Moreover, Miami's quasi-tropical climate resembled Cuba's.

Those who had come in the past as exiles belonged to the more politically active segments of Cuban society—

for example, the opposition to Gerardo Machado in the early 1930s and to Batista in the 1950s—but not this time. This was a different type of exodus, far greater in numbers and consisting of the well-educated upper and middle classes and their families; unlike their predecessors, they had left everything behind. More significantly, their concentration in Miami, then a resort town catering mainly to winter tourists, would eventually offer them the opportunity to lay the foundations of a thriving Cuban enclave.

> My arrival, November 11, 1960, alone, was probably one of the saddest moments of my life. I had $210 in a check hidden in my coat. My wife and my child arrived the next day. I was lucky that I was hired as a clerk—I was a lawyer and a CPA in Cuba. I was hired as a clerk at Washington Federal Savings and Loan. (Author's interview with banker Bernardo Benes)

As more and more exiles came, they tended to settle in the then-depressed areas of Miami's southwest section, where rents were low. South Florida, a racially segregated community, had never witnessed such an incursion of often destitute ethnics moving into "Anglo" neighborhoods; these foreigners were very different from the free-spending Latin American tourists who stayed in Miami Beach's hotels. Their sudden impact on the community was greeted with mixed emotions by the established residents, who perceived the newcomers as clannish and loud. Like most immigrants who come to America, the Cuban exiles met with some resentment.

> Some people resented our presence here because we speak a different language, we were talking too loud, we didn't have enough money and, when we rented an apartment, a two-room apartment, maybe seven or eight relatives would move in. So, they had signs saying: "No Cubans, no pets, and no children." (Author's interview with banker Luis Botifoll)

The exiles, in fact, *were* clannish and loud. In those days, several nuclear families often pooled their resources and crammed into small apartments until each family was able to afford a place of its own. And they were also conspicuous. During the day, hundreds gathered downtown to share the latest news from Cuba and to exchange information about available jobs; at night, they visited with friends and sat on their porches seeking relief from Miami's heat. From the very start, the emigrés showed an all-consuming desire to stay in touch with each other and, to the extent they could afford it, keep alive their traditional way of life. By the end of the Survival Stage, an embryonic exile community was already emerging within Miami.

A Cuban Boy Adjusts to America

Gustavo Pérez Firmat

Gustavo Pérez Firmat was eleven years old when he fled
Cuba with his family in 1960. In this firsthand account of
his early days of exile in the United States, he describes the
two main concerns of his parents and their friends: the
struggle to survive in a new country and the fierce hope that
Fidel Castro would be quickly overthrown. Young Gustavo,
however, had his own struggles: learning English and fitting
in at his new school in America. He describes the culture
shock of the early days as he learned the ways of America
while at the same time tried to retain his identity as a
Cuban boy. Pérez Firmat is professor of humanities at Co-
lumbia University in New York City and the author of *Life
on the Hyphen: The Cuban-American Way.*

When we got off the ferry on the morning of October 25,
[1960] we were met by my parents' friends Arturo and
Orquídea. Arturo was a *comisionista*, a sales rep for American food companies. In January 1959, when [Fidel] Castro took over, he and his wife had been in the United States
on business, and they had decided to stay in Miami rather
than go back to Cuba. While we drove over the mile-long
bridges that connect the Florida Keys to the mainland, my
father and his friend took stock of the situation. Arturo
talked about the rumors that a U.S.-sponsored invasion was
imminent. My father wanted to find a place to stay for a

Gustavo Pérez Firmat, *Next Year in Cuba: A Cubano's Coming-of-Age in America*.
New York: Anchor Books, 1995. Copyright © 1995 by Gustavo Pérez Firmat. Reproduced by permission of Doubleday, a division of Random House, Inc.

few weeks until the situation in Cuba became clearer. Sitting between the two men in the front seat of the car, I listened quietly to their conversation and wondered whether my father would be part of the invasion.

The Leamington in Downtown Miami was a modest, four-story hotel that had been built in the 1920s. The sand-colored building with the maroon trimmings stood on Northeast First Street across from the Greyhound bus station, only a short walk from Gesu Catholic Church, Bayfront Park, and the soon-to-be-famous Tower of Liberty, which housed the immigration and naturalization offices. My parents rented two connecting rooms on the second floor, one for my brothers, my sister, and me, and the other one for them. In a few days we would be joined at the hotel by other family members—my two grandmothers, various cousins and aunts and uncles, and several sets of godparents and their children. Although there must also have been Americans staying at the Leamington, for a while most of the guests seemed to be Cubans I knew from Havana.

Once at the Leamington, we fell into a routine. Every morning my mother and my aunt Mary would take a group of us children to the corner drugstore for breakfast; then we would walk to Gesu Church for mass, return to the hotel and play in the lobby for a while, have sandwiches or a hamburger for lunch (in those days you could buy a hamburger at the Royal Castle on Flagler Street for a dime), and spend the afternoon at Bayfront Park, which we called *el parque de las palomas*, Pigeon Park. In the evenings, while the grown-ups gathered in the lobby to talk about the invasion, the children played canasta or bingo in our rooms. Sometimes my uncle Mike would take some of the older children aside, sit down with us in a corner of the lobby, and pass the time away by explaining evolution. His favorite prehistoric ancestor, or at least the one I remember most vividly, was *Australopithecus prometheus*, which he pronounced as if it were a Spanish word.

Bored and Bewildered by Miami

For my brothers, my sister, and me, our first couple of weeks of exile were a mix of boredom and bewilderment. Since the Leamington wasn't a resort hotel like the ones we were used to, there wasn't much to distract us from our parents' constant conversations about our uncertain future. Only a few days before, we had been rich Cubans; now we were homeless exiles. My father said that we couldn't stay at the Leamington indefinitely, since the little money he had in the bank would soon run out, but he wasn't sure what else to do. For a while he talked about going on to Crowley, Louisiana, where his rice-grower friends could get him a job. But what was the point of moving so far away when Castro's overthrow might be only days or weeks away? Old enough to realize that this trip wasn't just another vacation, I didn't know what it was. I remember that my sister, Mari, sometimes would start whimpering, "I want to go back to Kohly, I want to go back to Kohly"—the neighborhood in Havana where we lived.

After nearly a month at the Leamington, my father put a $1,900 down payment on a house near Coral Gables, in the area that Cubans later called *la sagüesera* (a hispanicization of "Southwest"), and which Americans came to know eventually as Little Havana. The house, previously owned by an elderly American couple, stood in the middle of a grid of identical two-story duplexes that had been erected after World War II. Although soon this whole area would be teeming with exiles, at the time, the only Cubans in the neighborhood lived down the block from us; our other neighbors were all working-class Americans who didn't seem to notice that their neighborhood was about to change complexion.

We moved into our new house on a Thursday; Monday morning, my brothers and I went off to the public school a few blocks away. We were about to enter a new world.

Starting School

With a gymnasium and cafeteria, basketball and volleyball courts, and several wings of bright cinder-block classrooms, Dade Elementary was the picture-perfect suburban school from the 1950s. Unlike the austere, high-ceilinged rooms of the Cuban school I had just left behind, my sixth-grade classroom had several bulletin boards, a full-color world map, and pictures of famous Americans. In the front of the class, an American flag hung at an angle from the upper left-hand corner of the blackboard. On one side, large windows looked out on a little patio with a couple of picnic tables where we did our art projects; beyond the picnic tables was Douglas Road Park. Because the desks weren't nailed to the floor as they had been in Cuba, we moved them around according to the activity. I did not miss the dark corridors and shadowy courtyards of La Salle.[1]

Mrs. Myers, my sixth-grade teacher, was fiftyish, tall and wiry, with short reddish hair and very thin lips that she tried to disguise by smearing them with lipstick. She wore pale short-sleeved blouses and circle skirts with flowered prints. A devout Presbyterian, she would come in every Monday and begin the week by summarizing the sermon she had heard in church the previous day. Because she was the first woman teacher I'd ever had, at first I didn't know what to make of her. She once stopped in the middle of one of her warmed-over sermons to ask if anyone in the class would prefer not to listen to it. Understanding her question as an honest inquiry rather than a veiled threat, I was the only kid to raise his hand, and as a result spent

1. The author's school in Cuba was run by the Christian Brothers of La Salle.

the rest of the morning in the cafeteria. Unlike the La Salle Brothers in Cuba, Mrs. Myers knew nothing about my family and seemed uninterested in finding anything out. Her job was to teach me and the other students, which she did conscientiously. At the time, I thought her crotchety and cold, but now I realize that, like many Americans, she lived in compartments, and teaching was just one of them. All I knew of her life outside school was that she went to church on Sundays; all she knew about mine is that we had just arrived from Cuba fleeing communism. Maybe that's all she needed to know.

Learning About America

Although in a few years most children at Dade Elementary would be exiles, in November 1960 I was the only Cuban in my class. When I wasn't trying to act interested in Mrs. Myers's Monday-morning sermonizing, I absorbed American culture. In civics I read the U.S. Constitution; in history I found out about the Boston Tea Party and Paul Revere; in English I learned to diagram sentences; in music I memorized the words to "The Twelve Days of Christmas" and "Far Away Places" (some of my classmates must have thought I came from a faraway place, but this didn't occur to me). The one subject I actively disliked was current events, which required a group of us to put on a newscast every two weeks. Every other Friday we set up a row of chairs at the front of the class and took turns acting as newscasters. Someone did news, someone else did sports, someone else did the weather; it was my bad luck to have to report on the Teamsters. Since I hadn't the slightest idea who or what the Teamsters were, come Thursday evening I would pore over whatever story I had found in the *Miami News* that week. On Friday morning I was a nervous wreck, my bowels boiled and my hands trembled, but when my turn came I regurgitated the story back to the class word for word, sentence for sentence, all the while not understanding a thing. After my first time, Mrs. Myers went out of her way to be complimentary. "Listen, class," she said, "I want you to notice how much effort Gustavo put into his presentation." She didn't know what a superhuman effort it was. I must have given a half dozen reports on the Teamsters, and throughout those months I never realized that the Teamsters were a trade union; whatever it was they did in those days, to me it seemed shady, and I thought they were gangsters.

For the most part, however, classes went smoothly for me in sixth grade, especially since I never had the painful experience, common to so many immigrant children, of being thrown into a classroom full of people who speak a strange, unintelligible language. For me and my brothers, as for other Cuban exiles, English may have been foreign, but it wasn't strange. As Havana's unofficial second language, English permeated my childhood. We watched American movies, drove American cars, consumed American products, and listened to rock-and-roll music. In school we had studied English since the first grade; at home my aunt Mary gave [my brother] Pepe and me weekly lessons, which I loathed but which improved my fluency. Since my grandfather Firmat had been a consul in the United States, my mother fancied that she spoke English like a native, which she didn't really, but she spared no opportunity to flaunt her considerable fluency. She spoke English in the car, at the beach, over the dinner table. When she wanted to speak to my father without being understood by the servants, she resorted to English (he always replied in Spanish). Already in Cuba my brothers and I were being trained to become American; without knowing it, our parents were grooming us for exile.

CHAPTER 2

Political Unrest and the Next Waves of Immigration

COMING TO AMERICA

The Bay of Pigs Invasion

Harold Feeney

The 1961 Bay of Pigs invasion in Cuba by U.S.-trained forces was a disaster and an embarrassment for the United States—and a death warrant for many of the members of Brigade 2506, the Cuban exiles who volunteered to try to overthrow Communist dictator Fidel Castro. Harold Feeney, a retired intelligence officer, participated in the Bay of Pigs operation and later helped choose brigade members for armed forces commissions. In the following selection, Feeney interviews twenty of the surviving members of Brigade 2506 in Miami, twenty-five years after the invasion. The brigade members, still a tightly knit group, reminisce about their roles in the attack and talk about the dwindling of their dream of returning to a Cuba without Castro.

It was like surviving the Charge of the Light Brigade. "Someone had blundered," as Tennyson put it. This was Brigade 2506, the Cuban exile force that went ashore at the Bay of Pigs on April 17, [1961]. In a nightmare of fighting against an overwhelming force, 103 in the ill-equipped brigade were killed and 1,189 were taken prisoner. Four U.S. pilots foresaw a massacre and, disobeying orders, joined with brigade pilots and flew into combat in lumbering old B-26s. They were killed, shot down over the Bay of Pigs by [Fidel] Castro's fighter planes. In an international embarrassment to the United States, the prisoners were paraded before television cameras and the diplomatic corps in Havana. They languished in a Cuban prison until

Harold Feeney, "No Regrets—We'd Do it Again: The Veterans Speak," *Nation*, April 19, 1986, pp. 550, 554–57. Copyright © 1986 by The Nation Magazine/The Nation Company, Inc. Reproduced by permission.

being freed in December 1962, when President [John F.] Kennedy arranged payment of $53 million in food and medical supplies.

Who were these survivors and what has become of them . . . ? What happened to the secret agents trained by the Central Intelligence Agency to operate in Cuba to prepare an underground network prior to the invasion? Who do they think made the "blunder," and what lessons do they feel they have learned?

Brigade Was Carefully Trained

On a recent trip to Miami, I interviewed twenty of the surviving brigade members. At the time of the invasion they ranged in age from 18 to 40 and were from varied social and economic backgrounds. Most of the secret agents were between 19 and 23 years of age. The C.I.A. had put the latter through a rigorous screening process which included polygraph examinations, high-security-clearance investigations and tests for intelligence and physical ability.

A senior U.S. intelligence officer commented: "I wish the C.I.A. were as exigent in selecting its own agency personnel." Of the eighty-two agents, seventeen were either caught and executed or killed trying to escape. The others managed to make their way back to the United States. In addition to carrying out assigned tasks of espionage and sabotage, they trained many anti-Castro Cubans, who in turn came under C.I.A. control. Many of those local agents were killed when the invasion failed. Some escaped to Florida and, although not official members of the brigade, they are regarded by fellow exiles as heroes. A few of the regular agents and those they trained continued to work for the agency, but after the missile crisis of 1962[1] their missions to Cuba were limited to intelligence gathering. In

1. a thirteen-day standoff between the United States and the Soviet Union over Soviet missiles installed on Cuban soil, pointed directly at the United States

1964 some forty-two brigade members participated in a
C.I.A. operation to support then-Congolese President
Joseph Kasavubu against a communist incursion from Tan-
zania. Two brigade pilots were killed during the fighting.

The Brigade Is Broken Up

The brigade remained intact in Miami; the 1,800 survivors
were stunned by what had happened to them but remained
convinced that the U.S. government would soon use them
again in a liberation effort. That belief was enhanced when
President Kennedy reviewed them at the Orange Bowl on
December 30, 1962. Their commander, Dr. Manuel Ar-
time, presented the brigade flag to the President. The stadium cheered wildly when Kennedy promised them he
would soon return the flag to them in a "free Havana."

But it was not to be. After the October missile crisis Kennedy promised the Russians he would not intervene in Cuba,
and the brigade became a political embarrassment to the
President. He asked Joseph Califano, at the time a political
adviser on Defense Secretary Robert McNamara's staff, to
break up the brigade's leadership. Califano delegated the job
to Col. Alexander Haig, who arranged commissions in the
U.S. armed forces for more than 150 of them and found
good jobs or educational opportunities for others.

About half of those who received commissions were dis-
charged after a few years, but sixty-three of them went on
to serve with distinction in Vietnam. Of those, four were
killed in action and three wounded. "We could see the irony
of fighting what was perceived to be a Communist threat
halfway round the world while our nearby homeland was in
the iron grip of Fidel Castro," recalled Maj. Modesto Cas-
taner, now retired. "But in our frustration we were eager to
fight Communists wherever they might be."

A few of the C.I.A.-trained agents, however, refused to
abandon the fight against Castro. They joined independent

groups of exiles dedicated to carrying out operations inside Cuba whenever feasible. Without the knowledge of the C.I.A., according to them, they conducted sabotage in Cuba and harassed Cuban diplomats in Mexico and other countries. Those activities created a problem for the Federal Bureau of Investigation, which is charged with enforcing U.S. neutrality laws. The Bureau made a concerted effort to prevent illegal exile activities directed at targets inside as well as outside the United States. As one F.B.I. agent told me, "We were sympathetic to the cause of a free Cuba but could not condone illegal acts." Brigade members did not approve of acts of violent protest in the United States, believing the adverse public reaction would be counterproductive.

With respect to operations outside the country, the C.I.A. had done such a good job of training the agents to work clandestinely that few were intercepted. Nestor Tony Izquierdo, head of a Cuban exile group called the National Liberation Front (F.N.L.), learned that one of his colleagues had been jailed in Mexico for activities against the Cuban Embassy. In March 1976, Izquierdo flew to Mexico and, disguised as a police officer, entered the prison and liberated his comrade. During the Nicaraguan revolution he was killed fighting as a volunteer against a rebel group that he identified as a Castro-trained communist faction, leaving a widow and twin sons. To the brigade and the exile community he is a hero and a martyr.

Secret Activities Continue

In 1967, Castro's chief lieutenant, Ernesto (Che) Guevara, was in Bolivia exhorting the peasants to revolt. One of the brigade's former agents, who does not wish to be identified, said he paid his own way to Bolivia and volunteered to help Bolivian authorities track down Guevara. The C.I.A. and U.S. military advisers had trained Bolivian troops in counterinsurgency techniques, but, according to David Atlee Phillips, a top C.I.A. official, that was the only official U.S. involvement. A peasant woman revealed the place where Guevara was hiding. Phillips also said the agency wanted Guevara alive, but the Bolivian military insisted on executing him. The former brigade agent, who had talked to Guevara at length, was in the camp when the revolutionary leader was shot.

Robert (Tico) Herrera, one of the anti-Castro exiles who had been trained by brigade agents in Cuba, had also been one of Castro's lieutenants. He joined Cuban Representation in Exile (RECE), a group founded by Jose Bosch Lamarque, then an executive of the Bacardi rum company. Based in Florida, Herrera and a team of ten men made numerous clandestine forays into Cuba, evading Castro's security forces and, on the return trip, . . . Herrera was killed in an ambush in 1969 in Pinar del Rio Province.

Another who continued his activities was Alonso (El Curita) Gonzalez, a former Protestant minister. He was captured and escaped twice. In a desperate effort to get his wife and child out of Cuba, he learned to fly in Miami and in 1967 piloted a light plane to a remote airstrip in eastern Cuba, where his wife and child waited. But an informer had tipped off the authorities: Gonzalez was arrested and executed on the spot.

One of the most successful exile groups, known as Comando Mambisi, drew on the expertise of the C.I.A.-trained agents and operated several years after the invasion. In 1964, some of its members sabotaged the Matahambre nickel mines in Pinar del Rio. That same year another anti-Castro group, called Comandos L, infiltrated Cuba and exploded a mine against the hull of a Soviet merchant ship in Havana harbor. When one of the group's members, Tony Cuesta, faced certain capture, he attempted to kill himself rather than endanger his fellow agents. Although he exploded a grenade two feet from his head, he lived, losing both eyes and a hand. After spending eighteen years in Castro's harshest prison, he was freed and now resides in Miami.

No Risk Too Great

The story of Brigade 2506 is one of valor in combat and in the lonely business of being a secret agent. "How would you feel if your country was in the hands of a Communist dictatorship and you were on the outside? What chances would you take?" one of the members asked me.

In eastern Cuba just before the invasion, Rodolfo (Sea Fury) Hernandez volunteered for an important mission, although he was told his chances of surviving it were only one in ten. He knew he was most familiar with the terrain to be covered. He now works for the U.S. Postal Service in Miami and is a lieutenant colonel in the U.S. Army Reserve. "Yes, I'll be ready if they call me," he told me.

The four pilots who died trying to save the beachhead occupy a special place in the hearts of brigade members, who also feel a bond with other U.S. agents, from the C.I.A. and U.S. Navy Intelligence, who risked their careers and sometimes their lives for the cause. To this day those agents are referred to by their old code names—Pecos Bill, Quixote and Tobacco.

Former Brigade Members Are Close-Knit

Under the leadership of Miguel M. Alvarez, who became president of the Association of Combatants of the Bay of Pigs in 1978, former brigade members adopted a policy of giving international support to any organization fighting Cuba-directed actions worldwide. . . .

The former secret agents meet at irregular intervals, but each December there is a dinner in Miami for all members from the United States and abroad. At [one] dinner, Santiago Morales, . . . who spent eighteen years in a Cuban prison, joined his comrades in an emotional reunion. He had not been executed, he said, "because I was only 18 when I joined the brigade as an agent and looked like a young boy. When I was caught I had been operating alone and they could not relate me to a specific incident."

Most of the brigade members, now middle-aged, have settled down to life in the United States, where they have pursued successful careers, particularly the former agents. They include doctors, lawyers, engineers, a Florida State Representative, a vice president of the World Bank, an Army general, a vice president of Eastern Airlines and a host of successful businessmen. One [was] chief of President [Ronald] Reagan's bipartisan advisory commission on Radio Marti. They say they are willing to fight again under the right circumstances, but some have reasons different from those they had [in 1961]. Captain Eduardo B. Ferrer was one of forty-four pilots and air crew members of Brigade 2506 and a hero of the air battle. Now a senior pilot with Eastern Airlines, he says he would fight again for the cause of liberty for his former homeland, but his life and work would remain in this country. He had flown for Cuba's civil airline, Cubana de Aviacion, and is the only commercial pilot ever to hijack his own aircraft to defect from a Soviet-bloc country.

Survivors Blame Kennedy

Ferrer, like all the brigade survivors I interviewed, feels no bitterness toward the C.I.A. Debates may continue elsewhere, but for the brigade leaders the blame rests with one man, President John Kennedy. Ferrer says Kennedy made several mistakes, the most egregious being the cancellation of a second planned air strike, which was to have completed the destruction of Castro's military aircraft on the ground. The change in plans allowed Castro's remaining airplanes to sink the invading ships and pin down the beachhead. Kennedy also insisted on a more difficult and dangerous nighttime assault and made an eleventh-hour change in the planned landing site to a much riskier one. Moreover, the President insisted that the C.I.A., rather than the military, direct planning and operations.

Ferrer agrees with Adm. Arleigh Burke, then the head of the U.S. Navy and a member of the Joint Chiefs of Staff, that cancellation of the air strike was tantamount to a death warrant for the brigade. When the invasion was in its final throes, Admiral Burke begged the President to let him save the effort with a few Navy aircraft from a U.S. carrier that was in sight of the battle. Kennedy refused, saying he did not want the United States to be involved. Burke cried out in frustration, ". . . We are involved, Mr. President, and there is no way we can hide it!" In 1980 Burke told brigade leaders that the invasion taught one not to accept without question orders from a national leader because of being overawed by his position. "We should have questioned his judgment when we saw he was wrong."

Hope for Deposing Castro Fades

Brigade association president Alvarez believes that the United States should not undertake programs that could become half-measures. "Half-measures are worse than none because they nullify other options. I resent the fact that those who did the fighting were not allowed to participate in the planning."

Now brigade members live with a dream tempered by reality. As time passes they realize that their chances of deposing Castro have become remote. Some find this truth painful. Jose Basulto says: "I am financially successful, with all the worldly possessions I need. Yet I can never be completely happy until Cuba is liberated. We made a tremendous psychological commitment and this has caused a great deal of stress for years." The lesson of the

Bay of Pigs, according to Basulto, is that the United States must know what it wants and go for it openly instead of using covert operations. "The C.I.A. was not entirely competent, but they are not to blame. It was the White House. The saddest message I received from the C.I.A. on my radio was the final one on April 17: 'Do not transmit any more. SURVIVE.'"

At almost the same time on the beachhead at Playa Giron, the brigade military commander sent a last emotional message to the C.I.A. base in the United States: "I will not be evacuated. We shall fight to the end. This is where we have to die. We shall never abandon our homeland.". . .

In their heart of hearts they surely know that [another] invasion of Cuba is not likely to occur. What might have taken only a battalion of marines in 1961 would now require as many as seven divisions and entail immense losses: it would be a Pyrrhic victory. Also, in the absence of a casus belli,[2] the dream of overthrowing Castro remains what it was twenty-five years ago—a dream.

2. Latin for an act or event that provokes or is used to justify war

Cuban Culture and Religion in Little Havana

James R. Curtis

For the thousands of Cuban exiles who settled in Miami's Little Havana neighborhood after Fidel Castro seized power in Cuba in 1959, it was only natural to try to preserve their cultural and religious identity. In the following selection, author James R. Curtis describes how Little Havana has become a self-contained community for Cuban immigrants. He also discusses yard shrines, a by-product of both Catholicism and the Afro-Cuban religion of Santeria, which embody the religious expression of Cubans living in Little Havana. Santeria allows many Cuban Americans to hold on to memories of their life in Cuba, he says. Curtis is a professor of geography at California State University, Long Beach. He has undertaken considerable research on Santeria and has also coauthored *The Cuban-American Experience: Culture, Images, and Perspectives.*

In the summer of 1978 a brief article entitled "Neighbors Irate Over Family's Shrine" appeared in *The Miami Herald.* The story told of a group of residents in the predominantly non-Latin city of South Miami who feared that a newly-erected, seven-foot shrine in the front yard of a Cuban neighbor would lower property values. City officials called in to investigate found that the shrine was located too close to the front property line, and thus was in viola-

James R. Curtis, *Rituals and Ceremonies in Popular Culture*, edited by Ray B. Browne. Bowling Green, OH: Bowling Green University Popular Press, 1980. Copyright © 1986 by The Nation Company L.P. Reproduced by permission.

tion of municipal building and zoning laws. Confused and saddened by the turmoil created the Cuban family stated that the shrine had been built (at a cost of $1,500) in gratitude to Santa Barbara "for answering all of our prayers."

More than an isolated human interest story, the above incident is perhaps symbolic of the bicultural social adjustments, and urban landscape transformations, which have taken place and are continuing to occur in the greater Miami area as a result of Cuban in-migration. . . . The impact of such sudden and fundamental change in the pattern of ethnicity has profoundly altered both material and nonmaterial elements of culture in the region. Nowhere are these transformations better manifested than in Little Havana, a four-square-mile enclave of Cuban culture located a scant mile southwest of downtown Miami.

Life in Little Havana

Often referred to as "a city (or 'nation') within a city," Little Havana is the nucleus, the core, of Cuban life in Miami. Once a healthy middle-class Anglo neighborhood, dating from the immediate post–World War I era, by the mid-1950s it had deteriorated and was declining in population as urban growth and increased mobility opened up newer housing areas for the middle-class in the outlying suburbs. For the newly-arriving Cuban refugees this area was preferred in respect to having available and affordable housing units and vacant shops for potential business endeavors. It was also served by public transportation and near the central business district where social services and employment opportunities were most abundant. The neighborhood was reborn as "Little Havana" almost literally overnight. Although its function as the principal receptor area has declined in recent years as the Cuban population has grown in numbers and affluence, and has since spread out to other settlement areas, Little Havana remains in spirit, if not landscape, the traditional Cuban quarter.

In most important respects, Little Havana is a self-contained community which has evolved, by design, to suit the needs and tastes of its residents, and in so doing has embellished the landscape with a pronounced Cuban flavor. Along West Flagler and Southwest Eighth Streets (the latter known locally as "*Calle Ocho*"), the two principal commercial strips which cut through the district, a full complement of goods and services is offered which cater to the Cuban population. If so desired, a Cuban who lives in Little Havana and speaks only Spanish, could shop, dine out, be medically cared for, attend churches, schools, shows and theaters, die and be buried without a word of English being uttered.

The commercial landscape of Little Havana reflects in both vivid and subtle ways this impress of Cuban culture. From the older stucco buildings of Spanish and art deco styles, and from the small shopping plazas which have been built of late, neon store signs flash "*Joyeria*," "*Ferreteria*," "*Muebleria*," "*Farmacia*," "*Mercado*," "*Zapateria*,"[1] and so on. One frequently encounters small groups of three and four gathered at the countless vest-pocket, open-air coffee counters to sip the syrupy-dark, bittersweet *cafe cubano* and consume fresh *pasteles* (pastry).

The newsstands and bookstores in the district display a plethora of Spanish-language books, magazines and news-papers, including *El Miami Herald* with a circulation in excess of 50,000. The acrid smell of cured tobacco wafts from the thirty or so small cigar factories located in the area where old men (*tabaqueros*) patiently roll cigars *a mano* (by hand). At Antonio Maceo Mini Park, on *Calle Ocho*, men play continuous games of dominoes on permanently-fixed tables and benches designed specifically for that pur-pose. Fresh fruits and vegetables are sold in open-air mar-

---

1. Spanish for Jeweler, Hardware Store, Furniture Store, Drugstore, Market, Shoe Store

kets and stands which dot the district. The sweet smell of simmering garlic hangs heavy over the hundred-plus restaurants, featuring Cuban and Spanish cuisine, ranging from elegant supper clubs with valet parking to four-stool cafes.

Sense of Exile Lingers

The life and vitality of these places, however, stand in stark contrast to the somberness surrounding the Cuban Memorial Plaza, where flowers and wreaths are faithfully placed at the base of the Bay of Pigs monument in memory of loved ones who fell during that ill-fated invasion. To be sure, the landscape of Little Havana conveys a strong feeling of pre-revolutionary Cuba, but the sense of a people in exile remains pervasive. The existence of nearly one hundred officially recognized "municipalities in exile," which function as social and quasi-political organizations composed of former residents of particular municipalities in Cuba, attests to their vitality. Many of these groups, in fact, have converted houses and other buildings in Little Havana into meeting halls where lectures, concerts and dances are periodically held, and where informational and historical newsletters are published.

Thus, as befitting a people caught inextricably between two cultures, Little Havana is not an isolated community devoid of contact and consequence with the surrounding society and environment. Rather, in culture and landscape, it is a mixture of both Cuban and American influences. Cuban and American flags, for example, proudly bedeck the streets of Little Havana during national holidays of both countries. Cuban (grocery) shoppers may patronize the neighborhood Winn Dixie or Pantry Pride supermarkets, and then walk to the back parking lot of these stores and barter with itinerant Cuban peddlers selling fresh fish, poultry, fruit and vegetables. Teenagers sip on *batidos* (exotic fruit milkshakes) from Cuban ice cream shops and eat *grandes macs* from the local McDonald's. In language as well, especially among the younger Cubans, one now hears a curious mixture of Spanish and English ("Spanglish," as it is known). Signs on some store windows, for example, announce "Gran Sale." Young people may be heard shouting to one another, "*Tenga un* [Have a] nice day."

Although the housing area of Little Havana has been significantly up-graded and changed as a consequence of the Cuban tenure, the residential landscape is not nearly as "Latinized" as the commercial strips in the district. In fact, a quick drive through the area would probably leave the impression that it is largely indistinguishable from neighboring Anglo residential areas. Yet, upon closer inspection, differences unfold. Fences, for example, now enclose many front yards, and wrought iron and tile have been added to some houses for decorative purposes. Even these characteristically Hispanic features, however, remain relatively minor in comparison to what one might expect to find in most Latin communities. If anything, one is impressed more by how little these embellishments reflect the fundamental replacement of culture groups which has occurred in the area. This observation, however, is somewhat misleading, for it fails to include the single most conspicuous landscape element which clearly distinguishes Little Havana from non-Cuban residential areas.

Yard Shrines

If the Cuban family in the story recounted at the beginning of this article had lived in Little Havana, it would not have aroused the resentment, or even stirred the curiosity, of neighbors over the construction of its yard shrine. City officials would not have been brought in to search for some minor infraction of local building or zoning laws to force its removal. More commonplace than exceptional, there are literally hundreds of yard shrines gracing the cultural landscape of Little Havana.

The shrines may be found anywhere in the yard area—front, back or along the sides—although the front yard, especially near the sidewalk, appears to be a favored location. Regardless of placement, however, the front of the shrine always faces the street. Since these are personal shrines, built to suit the religious needs and preferences of individuals, no two are exactly alike; diversity is the standard. In size, the shrines range from about two to ten feet in height, and two to six feet in width. Most are rectangular in shape, although octagonal and circular structures are not uncommon. The most frequently used building materials include brick, cement, stone and glass; wood is rarely, if ever, used except for trimming. Exterior walls, though, are often stuccoed or tiled. A single cross may adorn the top of a shrine, and use of latticework and other forms of ornamentation are occasionally found, but in general the degree of exterior embellishment is more austere than ornate.

Regardless of size, materials used, or shape, the interiors of the shrines remain visible through either sealed glass side panels or a single glass door enclosing the front of the sanctuary. Pedestalled inside, usually on an elevated platform or altar, stands a single statue. At the base of the statue, and occasionally on a small stairwell leading to the base, one often finds an utterly baffling array of items, including, for example, fresh-cut or artificial flowers, candles, crucifixes, jars of leaves, bowls of water, beads, stones, miniature figures of men or animals, and other assorted paraphernalia.

Shrines Reflect Catholicism and *Santeria*

The statues themselves are of Catholic saints, the Madonna and Jesus, each identifiable (at least to the knowing eye) by sex, colors, adornment, and particular symbols, such as a cup, a cane or a cross. By far, the three saints which are enshrined most commonly in Little Havana are, in order,

Santa Barbara, Our Lady of Charity (patron saint of Cuba), and Saint Lazarus. Other saints, particularly Saint Francis of Assisi, Saint Christopher and Saint Peter are also found, but with much less frequency. Likewise, shrines built in honor of the Madonna and Jesus are not nearly as numerous as those erected to the main three saints.

Santa Barbara is most often portrayed as a young woman dressed in a white tunic with a red mantle bordered with gold trimming. She wears a golden crown and holds a golden goblet in her right hand and a golden sword in her left. Our Lady of Charity is similarly represented as a young woman dressed in a white tunic. Her cloak, however, is either blue or white. She holds a child in her left arm. At her feet, seated or kneeling in a boat, are two or three small male figures looking reverently upward. Saint Lazarus is usually depicted as a bent and crippled man of middle-age, with open wounds and sores, supported with the aid of crutches. Two or three small dog figures often stand at his feet. This particular portrayal of Lazarus is not the image officially recognized or sanctioned by the Church; it has evolved from Cuban tradition.

Sacred elements in the landscape often convey much less religious context from which they spring than obser-vation alone would suggest. The religious beliefs which in-spire the construction of yard shrines in Little Havana are illustrative of this contention. Considering, for example, that a vast majority of Cubans are Roman Catholics, and that most of the shrines are built in apparent homage to saints, one might logically suspect that these shrines are erected by followers of the Catholic faith. This assump-tion, however, is neither entirely correct nor incorrect. In truth, many of the shrines are built by Catholics, but per-haps an equal number, if not more, are erected by follow-ers of a fascinating, syncretic Afro-Cuban cult religion called *Santeria*.

Santeria Has Roots in Africa and Cuba

The history of the West Indies is rich in examples of the spontaneous melding of European and African culture traits and complexes. This process of transculturation—in which different cultural elements are jumbled, mixed and fused—played an important role in the shaping of present cultural patterns in the region, particularly in the non-material aspects of culture such as language, music and religion. More notable examples of religious syncretism in the New World in which elements of Catholicism were combined with ancient African tribal beliefs and practices include *Vodun* (i.e., "voodoo") in Haiti, *Xango* in Trinidad and *Santeria* in Cuba.

Santeria, like other syncretic Afro-Christian folk religions, combines an elaborate ensemble of ritual, magical, medical and theological beliefs to form a total magico-religious world view. The *Santeria* religion evolved among descendants of the Yoruba slaves who had been brought to Cuba from Nigeria beginning in the sixteenth century, but particularly in the first half of the nineteenth century. These descendants—known in Cuba as the *Lucumi*—learned from oral history the tribal religion of their ancestral home. It was a complex polytheistic religion involving a pantheon of gods and goddesses called *orishas*. It was also colorful in its mythology. In many respects it was extraordinarily reminiscent of ancient Greek mythology. The African religion was rather quickly altered, however, as the Cuban *Lucumis* fell increasingly under the sway of the Spanish culture. Exposure to the Catholic religion, particularly its veneration of numerous saints, greatly influenced the nature of the emergent folk religion. In time, the Yoruba deities came to be identified with the images of Catholic saints. The *orishas* then became *santos* ("saints"), and their worship became known as *Santeria*—literally the worship of saints. Thus, to the *santero* (i.e., the practitioner of *Santeria*), a shrine may be built to house a statue in the image of a Catholic saint, but the saint is actually representative of a Yoruba god. It is exceedingly difficult to determine accurately, based solely on appearance, whether a yard shrine in Little Havana actually belongs to a Catholic or a follower of *Santeria*. In general, however, yard shrines built by practitioners of *Santeria* are more likely to contain non-traditional religious items such as bowls of water, stones and jars of leaves.

The followers of *Santeria* believe in a supreme god called *Olodumare, Olofi* or *Olorun*. He is thought to be a distant, lofty figure. Contact with this supreme deity is attainable only through the *orishals* who serve as intermediaries. Thus, worship of god-saints serves as the focus for formal and informal devotional practices; there are no subcults or special rites exclusively in honor of *Olodumare*.

The saints—who are known both by their Catholic names and their Yoruba appellations—are associated with specific colors, particular symbols or "weapons," such as thunder, fire or swords, and are considered to have the same supernatural powers ascribed to the African deities. Each is believed to possess specific attributes, which in total govern all aspects of human life and natural phenomena. A *santero* might seek to invoke the power, for example, of *Babalu-Aye* (associated with Saint Lazarus), god of illness and disease, to cure a particular ailment, or *Orunmila* (associated with Saint Francis of Assisi), god of wisdom and divination, to bestow knowledge. Others, purportedly, can assure success in a job, ward off an evil spirit, bring back a former lover, and so on.

Santeria Has Important Functions for Exiles

The numerous deities, however, are not all venerated equally; some are more favored than others, often leading to the formation of a special subcult devoted to a particu-

lar god-saint. In Cuba, as in Miami now *Chango* (associated with Saint Barbara), god of fire, thunder and light-
ning, is the most popular of all the *orishas*. *Chango* rep-
resents a curious form of syncretism involving a change of
sex from the male Yoruba god to the female Catholic saint.
Oshun (associated with Our Lady of Charity, patron saint
of Cuba), god of love, marriage and gold, and *Babalu-Aye*
are also extremely popular in Miami. Seven of the most
revered and powerful *orishas* are often worshipped collec-
tively. This group is known among *santeros* as the "Seven
African Powers.". . .

The ritual and devotional activities of *santeros* are con-
fined, in most cases, to private residences. The more important functions, such as an initiation into the cult, a funeral, or a consultation in which some form of divination
is sought is presided over by a high "priest" of the religion, called a *babaloa*. Lesser orders of priesthood attend
to the more mundane rites and rituals. The rituals themselves are primitive, bizarre affairs, often involving the consumption of beverages concocted from exotic herbs and
roots, the use of incense, oils and foreign perfumes, drumming, dancing, trance inducement and animal sacrifices.
Many of the liturgical practices including phraseology
used in prayers and incantations, as well as various paraphernalia needed for ritualistic purposes, are also borrowed
from Catholicism. A *Santeria* priest might even suggest to
a follower that he or she attend a Catholic mass; in many
cases simply to obtain holy water or even a piece of the
consecrated host for use in a subsequent ritual.

The Expansion of *Santeria*

As surprising as it may seem *Santeria* today is neither a
predominantly rural nor a lower socioeconomic class phenomenon. Indeed, authorities on the religion confirm that
Santeria has permeated all racial groups and socioeco-

nomic classes in Cuba, and now in the Cuban community in exile. With the Cuban immigration to the United States, *Santeria* is known to be thriving in the larger cities where Cuban refugees have settled, including New York, Los Angeles, Detroit, Chicago and particularly Miami. A precise determination of the numbers of adherents to *Santeria* in Miami is virtually impossible to ascertain, since they do not build public churches or publish membership records. It is believed, however, that their numbers run into the thousands. One rough indication is provided by anthropologist William Bascom who estimated in 1969 that there were at least 83 *babaloas*, or high priests, practicing in Miami. This may be compared to Havana, which is the stronghold of *Santeria* with tens of thousands of followers, where Bascom estimated the number of *babaloas* at about 200 just prior to the Cuban Revolution. Perhaps a better indicator is the existence in Miami of over 12 *botanicas*, which are retail supply outlets catering to the *Santeria* trade.

By all scholarly accounts, *Santeria* is becoming increasingly popular among certain segments of the Cuban exile community. The reason most commonly cited for this kindling of interest is the fear of some Cuban refugees of losing their cultural identity through acculturation to the American way of life. Such a conversion would perhaps represent an attempt to maintain linkage to a more stable past in the face of rapidly changing values and lifestyles. Disenchantment with the Catholic faith is another factor also frequently mentioned as contributing to the apparent expansion of *Santeria* in the United States. In this respect, the Catholic church's questioning of the historical validity of certain saints who were popular in Cuba (such as Saint Lazarus and Saint Christopher), the elimination of many rituals practiced in Cuba, and just the size and institutionalized nature of the Catholic religion have reportedly prompted some Cuban-Americans to seek out alternative religious affiliation, including *Santeria*. Furthermore, the adaptive nature of the *Santeria* religion itself has apparently contributed to its expansion. [Anthropologist] Mercedes Sandoval, for example, concludes that: "Its intrinsic flexibility, eclecticism and heterogeneity have been advantages in helping ensure functional, dogmatic and ritual changes which enable it to meet the different needs of its many followers." Evidently one of the more important and attractive aspects of *Santeria* for the Cuban community in Miami is its function as a mental health care system.

In the process of change and modification as practiced in the United States, however, many African chants and dances, the use of certain herbs and roots and other medicinal and ritualistic elements have been abandoned. One of the more interesting adaptations, for example, involves a change in the Oil of the Seven African Powers, used in the worship of those deities. The "oil" is now available in *botanicas* in Miami as an aerosol spray. Directions on the side of the container read as follows: "Repeat as necessary. Make your petition. Make the sign of the cross. Air freshener, deodorizer."

Perhaps the apparent expansion of interest in *Santeria* among certain members of the Cuban exile community is only a transitional phenomenon which will subside, or die out completely, as the process of acculturation speeds ahead; which occurred, for example, in Italian-American cult religions. At the present time, however, as one follower of *Santeria* said, ". . . when we hear thunder in Miami, we know that *Chango* is in exile." Regardless of the future of this particular religious cult, the yard shrines and other contributions to the cultural landscape associated with the Cuban sector reflect the growing social diversity of this rapidly changing cosmopolitan city.

Operation Pedro Pan Brings Fourteen Thousand Children to the United States

María de los Angeles Torres

Operation Pedro Pan was conceived and organized by the CIA and Cuban dissidents in the United States and Cuba. The plan was developed because scores of Cuban parents who were unable to leave the island after Fidel Castro gained power wanted a better future for their children. So they sent them to "Never-Never Land," which was how Miami was viewed, and the children became known as the "Peter Pans." Only the lucky children were able to stay with friends or relatives, but most of the children spent time in camps, foster homes, and institutions, where they often experienced neglect and abuse. In the following selection, author María de los Angeles Torres, a Pedro Pan child, tells her own story as well as the stories of other Pedro Pan refugees. De los Angeles Torres is a professor of political science at DePaul University in Chicago. She is also the author of *By Heart/De Memoria: Cuban Women's Journeys in and out of Exile* and *In the Land of Mirrors*.

Silence would shroud my trip to the United States. I was to tell no one that I would be going alone. As far as my extended family knew, my parents would be leaving with their children. We weren't really lying to our relatives when we traveled to Yaguajay to say farewell—my parents were work-ing to obtain travel documents for the entire family. But my visa waiver was the only one they actually had in hand.

I knew that I would be flying in a plane, and that I would travel with my best friend, Xavier Arruza. Ameri-cusa, my kindergarten teacher, who had gone to Miami af-ter her school was shut down, would pick me up at the air-port. My parents told me she would take me to Sally and Joey's house, the children of Nenita and Pucho Greer, who were family friends.

We began to fill a suitcase with clothes, towels, and handkerchiefs. I would take a gray and red vinyl backpack, and my doll, Isabelita, onboard. On the morning of July 30 [1961], just before sunrise, we loaded the car. The sky was just beginning to turn an orange pink as we drove to the airport. Today, I look at a photograph taken by Xavier's father at the airport: five of us, standing, slips of paper bearing names and phone numbers of contact per-sons in Miami pinned to our clothes. I cannot remember posing for the picture. I am standing next to Xavier, with a worried look on my face. Yet I do remember the airport, my mother leaning down and hugging me, her last words: "*Báñate todos los días, que los americanos no tienen esa costumbre.*" (Take a bath every day, Americans do not have that habit.)

As I walked out to the runway, a guard stopped me, searched my backpack, and demanded that I turn over my doll to him. In those days, the government wouldn't allow people to take anything of value out of the country, so many parents stuffed jewelry inside children's dolls. The guard let me keep my doll after he shook it and could hear that it was empty. On the plane, I sat next to Xavier. As we took off I looked out the window, excited to be up in the air for the first time in my life. Some of the kids began to cry. As hard as I try, I cannot recall whether I did, too. The next thing I remember is landing, stepping out of the plane, down the stairs, and into the airport. Xavier was pulled aside; I never saw him again. However, I did find him, forty-two years later, and was able to talk to him and one of his brothers by phone. He remembers nothing of our trip. A way perhaps of forgetting his experiences after arriving, which he and his brother shared with me. Theirs the most difficult stories for me to hear.

First Weeks in America

At the airport, I was scared. I couldn't see above the many adults who started to surround us. I couldn't see Americusa. I didn't know what I'd do if she wasn't there. Some time passed, it seemed forever. Finally I saw her coming toward me.

Here my own memory goes blank. What I recall next are fragments of the Greers' house. A few years ago, a friend asked me about my foster home experience. I told him that I had won the Pedro Pan lottery: the Greers were welcoming and very concerned about my emotional state. Nenita recalled that I was afraid and withdrawn for quite a while and shy—a reversal of what I had been like before the trip. Nenita sensed my loneliness and did everything she could to alleviate it. I remember that she gave me a box of chocolates, which I hid under the bed and the ants got to it. She remembers that when she asked me about it, I told her that I was saving it for my parents who would arrive any day. I was going through a difficult time. I slept in a bunk bed with her daughter Sally. Nenita even set up a small table for us to eat so that I could relate to the children and not be overwhelmed by the adults. I learned to blow bubble gum and started practicing English words. Sally was protective and Joey was playful. But I was sad, and at night I would cry softly so that no one would hear me. It was the uncertainty: no one could say when my mother and father would come. When they called, or we got through to them, I found it hard to talk to them. Their voices were a painful reminder that I was not with them. I was barely six years old.

About two months after I arrived, Nenita started a difficult pregnancy. The doctor ordered bed rest, and she made plans to send me somewhere else. My mother had a cousin, Frances, who had seven kids and whose husband, Islay, had served in the U.S. Army. I was taken to her house. Pucho Greer occasionally came to visit and brought presents—a stuffed poodle, or candies. For the next two months, I was lost in the hustle and bustle of a home with so many kids. I started first grade in a public school in our neighborhood, which would later become known as Little Havana.

Reunited with Family

Finally, my parents received notice that their visa waivers had been approved. We weren't exactly sure when they could get a flight, but we knew it would be soon. I waited anxiously. On the day they were to arrive, I was not taken to the airport. When I got home from school, I found my mother and my two sisters at my aunt's house. My father, however, was not there. He had been pulled from the plane at the last minute. During the summer, the government had issued a regulation that no doctor could leave the island. A friend pulled strings and a few weeks later he was allowed to leave, but what I had hoped would be a joyous event was instead filled with sadness and anxiety. These emotions would come to define the way we would relate to all things Cuban, for there were still many relatives left on the island.

Throughout the years, I have often wondered why my parents were able to come relatively soon after me; why I was not taken to one of the camps, and my cousins, who left unaccompanied several months after I did, ended up first in the camps, and then spread out to foster homes in Albuquerque and orphanages in St. Louis. Why did some children never see their parents again? I knew that each family, indeed each child of the exodus, had a different story and that some of the differences concerned the choices their parents made. But I also suspected that some of the stories were about what choices were available to the parents. And these, of course, had to do with governmental policies. . . .

Many Children Went to Camps

Every unaccompanied Cuban child who arrived at Miami's International Airport, whether he or she went home with relatives or stayed with the Catholic Bureau, was given a card with the name of a social worker. Those who had relatives or friends waiting for them, like myself, left with them. The children without relatives or family friends were met by a man they only knew as "George." He would drive them to one of several makeshift overcrowded camps throughout the Miami area. . . .

The children would stay until they could be placed in a foster home or sent to other facilities across the country. These facilities changed as the numbers and needs of the program changed. The first children stayed at St. Joseph's Villa since it was the only child care facility operated by the Catholic Welfare Bureau. The Sisters of St. Joseph staffed it. It had twenty-six beds and cared for dependent children under the age of twelve. Others in Miami included a home donated by [former Miami mayor] Maurice Ferre, which came to be known as Casa Carrión, after the house parents who ran it for forty teenage boys. Another was the Saint Raphael Home, a two-building complex of apartments one-half block off Biscayne Boulevard in Miami, run by the Jesuit Brothers, which housed seventy-four boys. Father Walsh[1] eventually moved in, too.

1. Father Bryan Walsh was one of the organizers of operation Pedro Pan, and he served as a surrogate father to many of the children.

Kendall's Children's Home was opened for Cuban refugee children on January 7, 1961. Previously it had been the county's home for African-American children. The previous summer, the county had desegregated its children's facilities. Kendall was located in southwest Dade County; the Welfare Department loaned Catholic Welfare three buildings that could accommodate up to 140 boys and girls between the ages of thirteen and seventeen. At first it was run by lay parents and by the Ursuline Sisters, followed by the Piarist Priests and then the Marist Brothers.

Children's Camps Were Stark

In July 1961, as Kendall became crowded, teenage boys twelve to fifteen were moved to Matecumbe. It was also located south of Miami; it had been a summer retreat for priests and served as a summer camp for Catholic youths. Now it was turned into a receiving home and school for 350 teenage boys. Its capacity was augmented temporarily by adding tents. The Brothers of La Salle ran a high school, although priests from other orders participated in the teaching as well. In 1962, Father Walsh was ordered by Archbishop Coleman Carroll to consolidate the camps and move the kids to Opalocka in what had been a military station. Despite attempts to make it a welcoming place, the facilities were stark and conducive to being run as what they had been—a military barracks.

As the number of children entering the United States increased, more receiving centers were added. In October 1961, Florida City, the largest shelter, was opened. It was licensed to care for seven hundred children and was located about 35 miles south of Miami near Homestead. Girls of all ages and boys under twelve were housed in three rows of garden apartments; meals were served in three shifts and classes were held at an elementary school run by Sisters of St. Philip Neri from Cuba.

The experiences at the camps were mixed. On the one hand, the kids were together and, in comparison to those isolated in foster homes, they had camaraderie. But the facilities at Camp Matecumbe were stark; Alfred Schwartz, a former army commander described it as follows in a letter to HEW [Health, Education, and Welfare] secretary [Abraham] Ribicoff:

> I wish to inform you of a situation, which is inhumane and unless corrected immediately, will further lower the prestige of the United States among those we desire to help. Obviously no U.S. government inspection [team] has ever seen this camp. It "houses" over 400 boys in wooden shacks and tents. They sleep in three high bunks and each boy has a living and sleeping area of about 150 cubic feet. There are SIX (6) toilets and TWELVE (12) showers . . . there's practically no protection from the cold and heat. The camp is located in an isolated area which abounds in coral and rattle snakes, clouds of mosquitoes . . . instruction is poor and almost non-existing. . . . Many of the boys are ill. . . . It's surprising they do not ask what side the United States is on. . . . As a former Air Force officer and base commander, I was horrified by what I saw at Camp Matecumbe.

Siblings Often Were Separated

Father Walsh tried to make the camps more like home for the children, hiring Cuban staff and bringing in many of the Cuban priests who had left the island. But others like social worker Joan Gross saw it differently, observing, "Teenagers are the hardest hit by homesickness. They are old enough to realize that a reunion with their parents is not guaranteed. The best [antidote] to homesickness is rapid orientation to American ways."

Many Pedro Pan children I interviewed remembered those camps as lonely and terrifying places. Margarita Oteiza had worked in Kendall for a while after helping transport the children from the airport to the camps for several months. She told me that her heart could not take it. The children would climb all over her asking for their mothers. "They were so little," she recalled. She then signed up to work at Matecumbe.

Brothers and sisters were split by age and gender—a separation that would haunt even those who were eventually reunited in foster homes, for in the camps older siblings in effect became surrogate parents for the younger ones. The importance of this relationship was underscored in a letter sent to [First Lady] Jacqueline Kennedy by a young man who was sent to live with his uncle, while his brother went to the camps. The brothers were eventually reunited when his brother was old enough to care for Luis. But a new fear set in because now his brother was also old enough to be inducted into the army. Luis wrote to the First Lady: "I am writing to you this letter because I'm in great need. My parents are in Cuba, and I live with my brother, he is the only one around me who really likes me and takes care of me. What am I going to do without him?"

Scholarship Promises Are Unfulfilled

Friends and relatives also complained they were restricted from visiting the children in the camps. Mireya Robles wrote to President Kennedy asking for permission to see her best friend's children. A Children's Bureau staff analyzed the problem for the White House:

> On September 10 three children, Yolanda, María del Carmen, and José Casimiro, six, seven, and nine, arrived at Refugee Center Kendall. She [Mireya Robles] has been visiting them every day; she is a friend of the family. The mother superior has requested that she limit her visits to once a week. The writer wants the president to intervene and to insure that the children remain in Miami until their parents who are awaiting a visa waiver arrive in Miami.

The children's education was another issue of concern. Many Cubans had sent their children to the United States thinking that they would receive *becas* [scholarships] to school in this country. Many were disappointed to learn that there were no scholarships and that they would not attend boarding schools. Several adolescents from the Matecumbe camp wrote the U.S. government about this. Miguel de la Torre, Gerardo Ameijeiras, and Antonio Valdés Medina actually reached the president with their appeal for help in finding scholarships. They had left Cuba, they noted, to escape communism and study in the United States. Alfredo Lanier, today a member of the *Chicago Tribune* editorial board, remembered that his parents' instructions before he left had been to study so that he could return to Cuba well educated. "I was very disappointed because we thought that I would be getting a scholarship to study in a school. And Matecumbe was like military barracks. In reality, there were no scholarships. That's what my parents had been told."

Children Moved from Home to Home

As the number of arriving children grew, the Miami Catholic Welfare Bureau pushed to move the children in the receiving camps out. Therefore the children often went from family to family before a final home was assigned. For example, Carlos Erie, today a professor at Yale University, and his brother were separated upon their arrival in the United States. Carlos was sent to Florida City, his brother to Kendall. After about two and a half weeks, the brothers were sent to two different families; the families happened to know each other, so the brothers were able to stay in contact. But when the families realized that the boys were expected to be with them for more than a brief stay, they returned them to Catholic Welfare. Carlos recalls:

> We were kicked out. Then the real nightmare began. We were sent to a group home run by a Cuban family that

had no children. Their name was Amador. It was near the stadium on 7th and 20th. There may have been eight or ten kids. The number kept changing. We did receive and send letters, but they were so slow. We could not call, though. We were only given one meal a day. I have a curvature of the spine that has been linked to malnutrition during my teen years. I was never hit, but my brother was, because his drawer was not as neat as the man thought it should be. We used to make a little money on the side by selling the magazine *ZigZag* door to door. There was little supervision and we used to roam the streets a lot. I did go to school during this time. We finally got out. I am not sure how. My brother says he is the one who contacted an uncle in Illinois and he was able to take us in. My mother tried to come out of Cuba but she was not allowed into the United States until 1965.

Alfredo Lanier was first taken to Matecumbe. Later he ended up being bounced around from relatives to foster care:

My parents decided to send me when the schools were closed. I went to a Catholic school, Los Maristas. My parents thought that this was going to be just a brief thing. They had to get the kids out of Cuba because they were in imminent danger of being abducted by the Soviet Union, or taken away from the parents. So there was a big rush, a big panic to get me out of Cuba. There was also a very firm conviction that it was only a temporary thing. That it was only three or four months, you would learn English or whatever and then come back to Cuba and resume life happily ever after. Of course, that didn't happen because I came here in February of 1962. Then the whole thing was shut down in October '62 with the Missile Crisis. And my parents didn't come here until '65. I really don't remember at all. It must be all in the back of my head somewhere. I don't remember getting to Miami. I know I went to Matecumbe. I had just turned fourteen.

After a three-month stay in Matecumbe, Alfredo himself made arrangements to go to a relative's home:

> I tracked down an uncle who had been living in the
> United States for many years. He was like our mythical
> uncle who had made it in the United States. Finally I
> managed to get to New York. Well, the reality was that he
> and his wife and daughter were living in an efficiency
> apartment. I stayed there for two years, but it was horri-
> ble. It didn't work out, they finally kicked me out of
> their home. And through the International Rescue Com-
> mittee and the help of one of my teachers they found an-
> other home for me. But that didn't turn out to be much
> better. It was a single guy, who used me as his personal
> maid. His parents and brother came from Cuba and then
> again I was kicked out. And after that I got a scholarship
> to go to a prep school. Another teacher helped me find
> another foster home, this one with an Irish-American
> family who put me to sleep in the basement of their
> home, but they treated me very well. I started working
> part-time at the library and one of the librarians, Mr. Al
> Linsky, one of the most important persons in my life,
> claimed my parents for me. By the time they came, three
> years had passed. . . .

Some Children Were Placed in Institutions

Two-thirds of the 8,000 children under the care of the federal government were eventually placed outside Florida in
various institutions including orphanages and religious
boarding schools. Now adults, the Pedro Pans' memories
of their placements are mixed. The shorthand way of describing these experiences were that you either received a
good or bad beca. The boarding schools seem to have been
among the *good becas*. Here children were treated like students in boarding schools. The letters received by Sara Ya-
ballí, who some called *Mamá* and others *Nuestro Ángel*
(Our Angel) describe the mixed experiences. A boy from
Matecumbe who was sent to Notre Dame in Morton Grove,
says that it was a "good *beca*," but that Christmas had

been very sad. Another in a Kentucky boarding school had a good one and resolved his loneliness by saying, "My responsibility now is to study for the future of Cuba."

But institutional placements were another story. Some remember stark, uncaring institutions run with little regard for cultural or personal differences, while others recall the camaraderie that developed among the various unaccompanied children. These may have been real boarding schools. The ones who seem to have had the hardest and even cruelest experiences were those placed in what had been orphanages.

By the early 1960s, the United States had been moving away from the institutionalization of parentless children in favor of placing children in foster homes. Most of the children in these institutions had been placed with foster families, but those left behind were often the hardest to place, and we can assume they were the most troubled. These state- and church-run institutions had been left largely vacant, so they could easily accommodate many of the newly arrived Cuban children. But these places were geared to hard work and severe, if not questionable, disciplinary methods. . . .

The U.S. government and the social service agencies caring for the children appear to have been more interested in the ideological battle against communism than in the children's welfare. The children's complaints to supervisors about mistreatments and abuse in institutions and foster homes often went uninvestigated if not unheard. Those complaints did not suit the mythology spun in the ideological battle of the Cold War about children who had been rescued from the evils of communism—their real experiences, to be lived and suffered silently.

Mariel Cubans Have Been Unjustly Detained in U.S. Prisons

Gary Leshaw

In 1980 Fidel Castro allowed more than 125,000 Cubans to leave for the United States by way of the port of Mariel, Cuba. This mass exodus came to be known as the Mariel Boat Lift. Although President Jimmy Carter promised to welcome the Mariel immigrants, several thousand were imprisoned and given no legal immigration status. In the following selection from testimony given to the U.S. House of Representatives Committee on the Judiciary, attorney Gary Leshaw describes the plight of the detainees. He describes how misunderstandings, mistakes, and petty offenses cast these Cuban immigrants into a virtual twilight zone for years on end without the benefit of due process. As a result of congressional testimony—and riots in two detention facilities—detainees were promised individual reviews and eventually released. Leshaw is a civil rights attorney now practicing in Decatur, Georgia, who represented the detainees for more than seven years.

Mr. Chairman, members of the Subcommittee, I am an attorney from Atlanta, Georgia. Over the past seven and a half years, my colleagues and I have represented the class-wide interests of the Mariel Cuban detainees in this country. We continue to do so today and are joined in our ef-

Gary Leshaw, statement before the U.S. House Subcommittee on Courts, Civil Liberties, and the Administration of Justice, Committee on the Judiciary, Washington, DC, February 4, 1988.

forts by others with the same deep commitment to change a process that has denied fair treatment and basic human rights to an entire social class. Over the years I have had the opportunity to speak with hundreds of detainees, meeting with many of them personally and communicating with many others by mail. My colleagues and I have litigated class-wide issues with respect to the immigration status of the detainees and with respect to prison conditions at the Atlanta Federal Penitentiary. Lawyers and non-lawyers alike have also represented individual detainees before INS review panels and are doing so at the present time. I have been involved in these efforts as well.

Mr. Chairman, at a press conference on May 5, 1980, President Jimmy Carter was asked about the first wave of Mariel Cubans then crossing the Florida straits to this country and long hoped for freedom. Said the President,

> [T]hose 400 [Cubans] plus literally tens of thousands of others will be received in our country with understanding, as expeditiously as we can, as safely as possible on their journey across the 90 miles of ocean, and processed in accordance with the law. . . . [W]e'll continue to provide an open heart and open arms to refugees seeking freedom from Communist domination and from economic deprivation, brought about primarily by Fidel Castro and his government.

Instead of freedom and justice however, literally thousands of Mariel Cubans soon found themselves in an Orwellian purgatory with little chance of escape in which the United States government took the position that as a matter of law, the Mariel Cubans were not really here. Ultimately accepting this legal fiction, the Courts have held that as excludable aliens, Mariel Cubans, not under criminal sentence, may be detained by our government indefinitely without benefit of due process. In the words of Judge Robert S. Vance of the Eleventh Circuit Court of Appeals speaking of Cuban detainees in Atlanta, "The government can keep them in the Atlanta pen until they die."

Immigrants Unjustly Detained Under Inhuman Conditions

Among the Cuban detainees in the Atlanta pen at the time Judge Vance issued his remarks was Rafael Ferrer-Mazorra. According to Mr. Ferrer, he had been working in a supermarket in late 1982 when a fellow employee convinced Mr. Ferrer to assist him in what turned out to be a drug transaction. Mr. Ferrer had not been involved with drugs previously and did not realize what he was getting into. His life in the drug trade ended after his one and only delivery, to an undercover agent. Due to the circumstances surrounding the way he was drawn into the drug deal and his lack of appreciation for what he was getting into, Mr. Ferrer wanted to plead innocent and go to trial. Instead, his attorney worked out a plea bargain. Because of his clean record, and the small amount of drugs involved, Mr. Ferrer received probation and dutifully reported to his probation officer from January, 1983 to March, 1984.

In that month, Mr. Ferrer received notice that he was in violation of his probation for failing to report to his probation officer. The notice was a mistake; Mr. Ferrer had been reporting and showed up at his revocation hearing with his evidence. The Judge, recognizing that a mistake had been made, postponed the hearing for a month in order that the records could be rechecked. As he attempted to leave, Mr. Ferrer was picked up by immigration officials and on March 22, 1984 brought to Atlanta where his odyssey in the "twilight zone" began. Married, Mr. Ferrer's wife Justa was expecting their first child the following month. Rafael subsequently met his son for the first time in the visiting room of the Atlanta Federal Penitentiary. Although Mrs. Ferrer, who is waiting for her husband in

Chicago, has secured an approved visa relative petition on her husband's behalf from the immigration service, Mr. Ferrer remains indefinitely imprisoned to this day [February 4, 1988], without the legal right to a hearing and facing the possible prospect of forced separation from his family forever, through deportation to Cuba, for a crime for which he was not even sentenced to jail. [Mr. Ferrer was approved for release from detention on April 7, 1988.]

Mr. Chairman, I find this state of affairs shocking and unprecedented in the recent history of our country. Today there remain some 3800 Cuban detainees in our country who are not serving criminal sentences but who remain imprisoned solely as a result of their immigration status. It is a fact that most of the detainees have committed one transgression or another. Yet all who were sentenced for crimes have completed their sentences. Many, as with Mr. Ferrer, were not even sentenced to jail time but were given probation, often having pled guilty to crimes at the advice of defense attorneys who did not appreciate the immigration consequences of such a plea. Nevertheless, over the years the United States government has consciously denied the detainees due process, declining to provide serious individual reviews and fair hearings to detainees in an honest effort to release those demonstrating no threat to society.

Instead, Mariel Cubans have, for a number of years, been locked up at the whim and caprice of the Immigration Service with little attention having been given to their individual cases. In examining the status of the Mariel Cubans in Atlanta some two years ago you perhaps foresaw the potential for recent events, Mr. Chairman, when you described the conditions under which the detainees were forced to live as "brutal and dehumanizing." You also stated that

> Moreover, as we saw during our visit the conditions under which these persons live are worse than those which exist for the most dangerous convicted felons. The conditions

of confinement at Atlanta do not appear to meet mini-
mum correctional standards. The measure of a Nation can
be seen in the way it treats the least advantaged among us.
By this measure our country has failed to meet any minimal standard of decency in our treatment of the Cuban
detainees at Atlanta. It is my hope that this report and its
accompanying recommendations will reverse the benign
neglect this issue has received in the public policy arena.

More recently, Judge Marvin Shoob, the United States
District Court judge who presided over the bulk of the
Mariel Cuban litigation, commented that:

After some years pass and we can view this more dispas-
sionately, there will be some real criticism of the decision
to detain these people in a maximum security prison
without a trial for up to six years.

And in a speech Judge Shoob commented that "the
moral of the Cuban situation is it *can* happen here."

Imprisoned Refugees Have No Voice

Although the plight of the Mariel Cubans has in the past received only minimal public attention, when circumstances
are fully set out, the injustice can be clearly seen. In 1984 a
disturbance was set off in the Atlanta Federal Penitentiary
when a detainee was taken to the segregation unit for insuf-
ficient reason. The government prosecuted two detainees as
"ringleaders" of the disturbance. After a trial lasting over a
week, the jury found both detainees not guilty in short order. The foreman of the jury, Mel Magidson, stated that "we
are ashamed of our government and the way things are going for those people." Juror Laquetta Goodman commented
that "they're not having a hearing, they don't have a voice.
Everybody in these United States should have a voice."

Perhaps the plight of the detainees is best expressed by
two of their own, Armando Sanchez-Garcia, who is now in
the federal penitentiary in Lompoc, California, as his fam-

ily waits for him in New Jersey, and Moises G. Hernandez, who has subsequently been released. Hernandez' artistic depiction is attached to these comments. Wrote Sanchez:

WE ARE

You see our faces
. . . look really mean.
We are scum.
We are worse.
We have no end.
But look deeply inside us . . .
And what do you see?
Are they hard faces?
Are they full of hate?
You know better than that!
It is pain and sadness.
It is crying and hurt.
It is the resentment of the victimized people,
The ones suffering, weeping, and hopefully waiting!

Threat of Deportation Sparks Uprising

Mr. Chairman, at the time of the Oakdale and Atlanta uprisings[1] the detainees in detention were undergoing a review process that might lead to the eventual release of many of them. The process, one in which INS officials, often border patrol officers, received one day's training before conducting detainee interviews, was not a very good one. Nevertheless, detainees were told that if they maintained good behavior, kept clean records, took educational courses in prison, performed their jobs, and maintained contact with their families or communities, there was a ray of hope that some might be released. In fact, at the time of the uprisings some 800 detainees by our count, perhaps more, had already been approved for release and were awaiting place-

1. The reopening of immigration relations between the United States and Cuba in 1987 meant that more than twenty-five hundred Mariel detainees could be deported and possibly imprisoned on arrival in Cuba. The threat of deportation led to two weeks of rioting at the Oakdale, Louisiana, and Atlanta, Georgia, detention facilities.

ment. And this was only at the beginning of the review process in which some two-thirds of detainees reviewed had received favorable recommendations.

On November 20, 1987 these detainees, not under criminal sentence, saw the door slammed in their faces. Having lived through years of neglect, denial, lies, and mistreatment by our government the detainees had done all that was asked of them in order to become eligible for release under a system in which they had been denied due process. Having done so they suddenly faced the prospect of the deportation of some 2500 of their number to Cuba, 2500 who would be forcibly separated from wives, husbands, children, and other loved ones, perhaps forever, without even the courtesy of a hearing. In short, this was the final straw, proving as the *Boston Globe* had noted many months before, that Jimmy Carter's promise to greet Cuban immigrants with "an open heart and open arms" had "become a mocking memory, a reminder that they lack even the basic constitutional rights granted to illegal aliens who sneak over the border."

Mr. Chairman, there will be much second-guessing as to the causes of the Oakdale and Atlanta uprisings and what might have been done to prevent them. In retrospect, I believe that the announcement by the State Department on November 20, 1987 set events on an unalterable course. Continuing a legacy of mistreatment and neglect, yet another governmental agency, this time the State Department, announced the prospect of mass deportations without once thinking of the necessity to take into account the individual cases of detainees who may well have already been released or had a chance to be released. Had the State Department and the Department of Justice even once bothered to consider the need for fundamental fairness, justice, and basic human rights, the events of recent months would have been avoided.

As the Most Reverend Agustin A. Roman, Auxiliary Bishop of Miami, had reminded us almost a year before the uprisings, deportations are not generally a solution for people who have grown roots in this country. The detainees, he said, "should be strengthened, giving them a moral base and principles that would allow them to recover their dignity as human beings and co-exist in a free society." Instead, the detainees were lied to.

The depth of the frustration endured by the detainees was felt by those counseling them. Early in his chaplaincy at the Atlanta Federal Penitentiary, Rev. Russ Mabry was sought out by a detainee. The man's wife who lived in New Jersey had just had a hysterectomy and his daughter was hospitalized with pneumonia. His wife had just written that they did not have enough money to get through Christmas. The detainee was very worried.

Said Mabry, who was to become one of the hostages during the Atlanta crisis:

> I had never before confronted that much pain. American inmates know why they're in prison, how much time they have and about when they'll get out. This Cuban didn't know when he was getting out or—if he got out— whether he would go live with his wife and kids or be deported. Underneath his pleasantness there was real rage. He had no control over his life.

New Review Process Has Flaws

Mr. Chairman, as a result of the agreements ending the uprisings a new review process, announced by the Department of Justice on December 11, 1987 is now in place. That process will hopefully result in the expeditious release of detainees who do not present a danger to society. I would be remiss however if I did not point out two gaping holes in that review process. First, although the Department of Justice promised each detainee a "full, fair and equitable review" of his or her case, nowhere in the process is there a provision for a fair hearing for the detainee. Obviously, detainees who are approved at the first level of review by INS upon file review or interview, have no need for a hearing. Those who are denied however, should have the right to make their case for release and not simply be subjected to a paper review by the Justice Department Review Panel called for in the new Review Plan.

Due process has been denied Cuban detainees long enough. Before any detainee is ultimately denied release or deported, it does not seem like too much to ask to allow him a hearing during which he can call witnesses in his behalf, confront the evidence against him and cross-examine adverse witnesses, be represented by counsel and receive a written determination on his application for release. The failure of the Departmen of Justice to provide such a mechanism renders the current review process less than full, fair and equitable.

As Congressman Pat Swindall has noted after a personal review of a number of detainee files:

> I might add that from my own observations, most of the files lack any predictable order, chronological or otherwise. Also, I have found that all too frequently, the files are incomplete. During my perusal of various INS detainee files, I found that on several occasions INS officials denied re-parole based on erroneous information contained in the files. In either case, some type of cross-examination of those individuals upon whom the INS's ultimate decision was based would have corrected these types of prejudicial human errors.

The second hole in the review process remains, Mr. Chairman, the inability of the government to actually release detainees who have been approved for release. By the Justice Department's own count there are at present some 1000 detainees already in that position. Adequate efforts and resources must be directed to the finding of sponsors and the release of detainees and the supervision of those who would benefit by assistance in their reintegration into society. Instead, there is currently much finger-pointing for the delay among the various governmental and contract agencies involved in the release process.

Living Conditions Should Be Improved

On a related issue, Mr. Chairman, we should not forget the condition of the detainees who remain imprisoned during the review process. After the uprisings there was an obvious need to restore order which justified a lockdown of detainees around the country for a reasonable length of time. I believe that reasonable length of time has now passed and that consistent with necessary security concerns, detainees around the country should be reintegrated into the general population unless a reason exists otherwise in a particular case. We remain quite concerned, Mr. Chairman, about reports of detainees in unreasonably harsh conditions around the country who are by their accounts living in overcrowded conditions and who are denied adequate medical care, personal hygiene, recreation, access to religious counseling, and visitation, among other things.

One detainee whom I saw personally at the United States Penitentiary at Leavenworth some three weeks ago, Arnaldo Rivas, wrote a letter within the past few days expressing his frustrations:

> We wonder how the [Bureau of Prisons] defines "NO RETALIATION" [as per the Oakdale and Atlanta agreements]. If our present living conditions are not a retaliation, then what is it? Why can't we have the same privileges we had? Actually, the death-row inmates have more privileges than we. Do you mean that being locked up 24 hours a day is not a retaliation? Do you mean that showers twice a week (5 min. each), being handcuffed whenever stepping out of our cells, no regular visits nor phone

calls, no religious services, not even being allowed to have a rosary, no work nor school, etc., is not a retaliation? Do you mean by recreation to go into small cages where not even pets should be? Do you mean by visits to have our families come from far away, spend several hundreds of dollars for just an hour a month without being able to kiss our loved ones? Do you mean by visiting room our own cellhouse? Where else has anybody seen a visiting room in a cellhouse? Who are we for you? Perhaps, modern slaves or human animals.

Mr. Chairman, on April 27, 1987 in remarks to the House, Congressman John Lewis, who has long been an advocate for fair treatment of the Mariel detainees, recalled the words of famed Soviet dissident Aleksander Solzhenitsyn. In Volume II of his work, the *Gulag Archipelago*, a history of Soviet internment camps, there is a chapter entitled "Hand Over Your Second Skin, Too." Asked Solzhenitsyn:

> Can you behead a man whose head has already been cut off? You can. Can you skin the hide off a man when he has already been skinned? You can.

What Solzhenitsyn was referring to was the additional detention imposed after a prior prison term had been served. Sardonically, the author continues:

> Oh, blessed are those pitiless tyrannies, those despotisms, those savage countries where a person once arrested cannot be arrested a second time! Where once imprisoned he cannot be reimprisoned. Where a person who has been tried cannot be tried again! Where a sentenced person cannot be sentenced again! But in our country [the Soviet Union] everything is permissible. When a man is flat on his back, irrevocably doomed and in the depths of despair, how convenient it is to pole-ax him again.

Personal Stories Are Shared

Mr. Chairman, in closing, I would like to return briefly to the impact of American policy over the past seven years on detainees and their families, particularly the children. Over the Christmas holidays a colleague of mine, Sally Sandidge, visited with Julia Martinez-Leon, a Cuban detainee in Lexington, Kentucky. Charged with possession of less than an ounce of marijuana, Ms. Martinez, and her detainee husband, Gerardo Mansur-Piniero, similarly charged, pleaded guilty and were sentenced to probation. As a result of their pleas INS detained both Gerardo and Julia, sending him to Atlanta and her to Lexington. Their two young children were put in foster care. Although Gerardo has recently been released, Julia remains in prison some four years later. She has not seen her children and seldom has news of them.

In the prison everyone calls her "Mommy" because all of Julia's thoughts and prayers are with her two little boys. For her the separation has been an agony. As my colleague sat in the visiting room with Julia watching other children play, tears rolled down Julia's cheeks. Approved for release, Julia remains imprisoned waiting for a release date.

[Writer] Charles Dickens wrote, "In the little world which children have their existence, there is nothing so finely perceived and so finely felt as injustice."

Also during the holidays we visited with some of the families of the detainees in Atlanta. Dorothy Diaz is a ten year old who has seen her father Ernesto Diaz-Gutierrez detained for three years after he completed serving his sentence. Every month during prayer visits outside the prison, Dorothy would call out to her father, "I love you." Every night Dorothy, with her mother, and little brother and sister, would walk to the prison and signal her father good night. This year [1987] the children wrapped empty boxes and put them under their Christmas tree.

Elizabeth Barrett Browning wrote:

But the young, young children, O my brothers,
    They are weeping bitterly!
They are weeping in the playtime of the others,
    In the country of the free.

For the children and families of the detainees indefinite detention has meant a never-ending nightmare of uncertainty and darkness. Some of the younger detainees themselves came over on the boatlift as children. Lazaro Chavez, age 20, now imprisoned at Leavenworth, was twelve years old when he arrived in this country. He has parents frantic with worry and grief.

John Quincey Adams, the sixth President of the United States and a one-time member of the House of Representatives, once stated, "America, in the assembly of nations, has uniformly spoken among them the language of equal liberty, equal justice and equal rights."

Surely our country can now find the moral courage to end this long tragedy of indefinite detention and broken lives.

CHAPTER 3

The Refugee Crisis and How It Changed Life in the United States

COMING TO AMERICA

U.S. Embargo Creates Dissent Among Exiles

David Rieff

During the early 1990s, the U.S. government wrestled with how to deal with Fidel Castro, concluding that the best way to force him out of power was to establish a trade embargo that prohibited sending anything to Cuba except food, clothing, and medicine. In the following selection, author David Rieff discusses the embargo and "political verticality," a position of steadfast support of the embargo adopted by many Cuban Americans. Rieff describes how the vertical position affected the actions and emotions of several prominent exiles, who often had mixed feelings about the embargo, knowing it would cause increased suffering for friends and family still in Cuba. The author is a journalist who covers humanitarian emergencies around the world. He has also written *Going to Miami: Exiles, Tourists, and Refugees in the New America*.

Because the end of a great hope rarely comes in one single, easily delineable moment, and because even the bitterest of revelations often engender, among those forced to confront them, a renewed determination to remain faithful to the feeling that has been betrayed or the cause that has been lost, it was not surprising that in Miami, in 1992, people were simultaneously registering the disappointment they felt over the fact that Fidel Castro had not yet fallen and clinging to the belief that their return was still imminent, Cuba's future still bright. True, Cuban Miami's nostalgia for the Havana of the past was shakier than it had ever been. The news brought by new arrivals from the island as well as by those who had traveled there on family visits was discouraging in the extreme. Since he had gone to Cuba in 1990 and 1991, Raul Rodriguez, who had traveled there out of love and obsession, found himself the bearer of too much of this bad news. He might spend his days in the high heat of Havana— "The only cool breezes I felt were at Varadero," he once told me ruefully—walking up and down the grand avenues of the bourgeois city taking photos of the houses in which his friends had lived as children, and, when he returned to Miami, he might make copies of these icons of that golden time and, at some considerable expense to himself, deliver as many of these images as there were requests for them. "Ninon," he could be heard to ask [his wife] on many a quiet weekend morning, "did you give so-and-so her house?"

Many Exiles Support Embargo

But though the absence of development in Havana during the sixties and seventies, the era in which the historic centers of so many Latin American and European cities had been ruined, meant that the facades that Raul photographed so assiduously had been more or less untouched, and, though they uniformly needed a bit of plaster and a coat of paint, it was easy enough to imagine them as they had been in 1959, Raul carried as many disturbing images home with him in his head as he carried heartwarming ones in his camera case. If he could give [his friends] Sandra Oldham and Tony Quiroga "back" their houses, he was also in a position to tell them just how changed Cuba was. And bricks and mortar were the least of it. The most disturbing news Raul had to impart was that the love for Cuba that stirred so many Miami hearts was not nearly so uniformly shared in Cuba itself.

This, too, made a certain bitter sense. After all, the material difficulties of present-day Cuba, however painful they were to the exiles, only demonstrated the criminality and folly of the Castro regime. In that sense, at least, Cuba's misery was Miami's vindication. Moreover, many in *el exilio* genuinely believed that things would have to get worse before they got better. The vertical position was that the U.S. trade embargo had to be maintained, even though it was clear that to call for this meant that one's own friends and relatives would suffer still further privation. Those who supported this view insisted that were things to improve slightly, as doubtless they would if the American government eased its stance, Castro's grip on power would only be strengthened. They cited the example of the United Nations sanctions against South Africa as a case in which making people's lives worse in the short run bad helped bring about change over the longer term. And they were consistent. Congressman [Robert] Torricelli's legislation,[1] so enthusiastically supported by the Cuban-American National Foundation,[2] called for a ban on all transfers to Cuba with the exception of food, clothing, and medicine. Under these provisions, it would have been illegal for a Cuban-American family in Hialeah or Kendall to even send a toaster or a fan to a relative in East Havana or Santiago de Cuba.

Disagreement Grows Among Exiles

There were, of course, dissenting voices in Cuban Miami. Arturo Vilar was a former newspaperman who now advised businesses about opportunities in various sectors of the Cuban economy. He was in many ways a typical member of the high-bourgeois exile, having lost everything to the revolution. Now, however, his dreams of return, his continu-

---

1. the Cuban Democracy Act of 1992   2. the pro-embargo organization dedicated to advancing freedom and democracy in Cuba

ing sense of being a Cuban exile and not either a Cuban-American from Miami or the resident of Madrid that he had been in the sixties, led him not to verticality but to the view that only a reconciliation between the exile and the regime would allow people like himself to return to Havana. In other words, he was for dialogue, and, like [anti-revolution activist] Francisco Aruca, whom he knew well, he was much resented for it. People said he was really advising companies on how to do business with the Castro government, a violation of American law. Vilar denied it. But that he was resolutely *dialogero* he did not deny, though, unlike his friend Aruca, he expressed his opinions with sad self-deprecation. When Raul Rodriguez once asked him whether he would go back to Cuba if he could, Vilar smiled sadly. "Oh, yes," he said. "I'd go back. . . ."

Even Vilar, however, was quick to acknowledge that most people in Cuban Miami were firm supporters of the embargo. "Personally, I don't understand it," he said. "It may be emotional on my part, but when I travel to Cuba, and I run into people who need *everything*, I just can't justify continuing the sanctions, let alone tightening them. I tell myself that I shouldn't be so emotional, but then I think, 'Why not? I'm a human being. And besides, what is this feeling I have for Cuba anyway if it is not something emotional?' It's a painful feeling. These days, knowing how hard things have become in Cuba, I have started to have a rough time enjoying all the things that I have here in Miami. It's not so bad when I'm alone, but when I'm with a group of people, at a dinner, say, with all the food and drink that we Cubans consume on such occasions, I often feel like gagging. I look at the table and I imagine the bare tables of friends in Miramar. We should be sharing our bounty with them, not pressuring the U.S. government to take away what little they have."

But, of course, the people at the Foundation who were

pressing for even more restrictions also believed they were acting out of love for Cuba. As Congressman Torricelli put it, the point of a more strictly enforced embargo was to "shorten the suffering of the Cuban people by isolating Castro and forcing him out." Nor was this view restricted to people who had left the island immediately after the revolution. To the contrary, some of the strongest support for the ultravertical position came from those who had come to South Florida since Mariel. A Foundation executive like Rene Jose Silva was being commonsensical when he told an interviewer that he found "a greater affinity for people who have left Cuba recently." In part, of course, his words were one more emblem of the breakup of the exile. People in Miami took Cuban culture for granted, he complained. But Silva was also right to suggest that the intransigent positions of the Foundation coincided with the gloomy sense of so many recent arrivals from the island that force was the only method of unseating Fidel Castro, and that to temporize with the regime in fact guaranteed its survival. As for reconciliation, the very idea was particularly repellent for those whose memories of Cuba were fresh, and as yet untouched by either life in *el exilio* or life in America.

Cubans Feel Hostility Toward Exiles

Even Arturo Vilar, though he might yearn for some breakthrough toward understanding between what he often liked to refer to as "the two Cubas," did not really expect his friends and acquaintances in Miami to share his feeling that the disparity between the lives people led in South Florida and the conditions those who had never left the island were now being forced to endure was more troubling even than Fidel Castro's continued rule. In any case, Vilar seemed persuaded that the continuation of the embargo would have the opposite of the desired effect; that anti-Americanism, not antigovernment feeling, would be the inevitable result in Cuba when Congressman Torricelli's Cuban Democracy Act became law. "There needs to be a synthesis between the exile and the island," Vilar told me over a lunch in a Spanish restaurant in Coral Gables called the Cenador de la Villa, where the richness of the food and the lavishness of the presentation would, in fact, have engendered a certain sense of guilt in a person far less committed than Vilar. "But if things continue to deteriorate in Cuba, I just don t see how that meeting can ever occur. The last few times I've been in Havana, I've been overwhelmed by the increasing hostility toward the exiles. People either want to come here or else they dislike us, or, human nature being what it is, feel both things. But when they hear that people in South Florida—Cubans like themselves—want the embargo continued, they can't understand what's going on. The hostility of the U.S. government is one thing. But to know that one's privations are counted as an accomplishment by one's relatives? That's incredibly bitter."

The problem was that, whatever Vilar might wish, it was also incredibly Cuban. Historically, the notion that one should compromise when fighting for a just cause had, for obvious reasons, had no place in the nineteenth-century wars of independence out of whose experience both Cuba's heroic myths and its political vocabulary had been forged. An episode like the "protest of Baraguá," in which [General Antonio] Maceo had refused a perfectly reasonable offer of a negotiated surrender to the Spaniards, had been more marking than the actual outcome of the incident, in which Maceo finally gave in and, under safe-conduct, quietly boarded a ship bound for Jamaica and exile. And if the streets of Havana were full of references to this heroic verticality, *el exilio*, too, exemplified a similar spirit. The true Cuban patriot, [independence leader] José Martí had insisted, must be as "prickly as a porcupine, and as upright as a pine tree." This was the attitude the eminent exile historian Carlos Ripoll had summed up in a famous essay on the Apostle of Cuban independence that he had entitled "The Noble Intransigence of José Martí." That intransigence could be encountered in a Communist slogan like "Socialism or Death"—what, after all, could that possibly mean after the fall of Communism except death, however heroic?—or in the exile insistence that there could be no dialogue, let alone compromise, with the dictator. "We want no compromise," Torricelli had insisted in a speech to a cheering Miami crowd, "we want a free Cuba now!"

Brothers to the Rescue Searches for Boat People

Susan Benesch

The U.S. trade embargo, coupled with the end of the Soviet Union's economic aid to Cuba, produced an unprecedented wave of Cubans who tried to escape the island in
rickety boats or rafts in 1991 and 1992. Hundreds died. In
the following article, author Susan Benesch describes her
search-and-rescue trip with Brothers to the Rescue, a
group of volunteer pilots who patrolled the waters between
the United States and Cuba, searching for boat people and
guiding the U.S. Coast Guard to their rescue. Benesch
shares stories of the survivors and tells of the volunteers'
despair at spotting an empty boat, a sign that the occupants had drowned. The author is a journalist and lawyer
who has worked as a refugee advocate for Amnesty International USA.

Floating below the plane on a vast, impassive sheet of sea-
water wrinked by six-foot waves and spattered with a million whitecaps, there would be one whitecap that wouldn't
go away, we were told. It would look like sea foam, but it
would be people, sick and sunburned, on a foolhardy trip
from Cuba to Florida.

They were surely there, because the Florida Straits were
relatively calm this week [in April 1993] and because about
50 Cubans climb into boats, makeshift rafts and inner
tubes off the northern coast of their isolated island every

Susan Benesch, "Brothers to the Rescue," *St. Petersburg Times*, April 24, 1993, p. 1A.

week as food, clothing and medicine grow scarcer.

Hundreds have died on the way. To save as many as possible, private pilots fly over the Florida Straits three times a week, looking for Cuban boat people and reporting their finds to the U.S. Coast Guard, which then rescues them. Most of the pilots are Cuban-American, all of them are volunteers, and they call themselves Brothers to the Rescue.

They meet at 7 or 8 A.M. on flight days at Miami's Opa-locka airport. A year ago they flew out at dawn, said Jose Basulto, president of Brothers to the Rescue, because they were competing against Cuban patrol boats that went after boat people to bring them back to Cuba and to jail for leaving without permission. This year, Basulto said, he has seen no patrol boats, apparently because Cuba is suffering severe shortages of gasoline. "Now we get to sleep a little later," he said.

Searchers Often Find Empty Crafts

Four planes flew Thursday, [April 22, 1993], piloted by three Cuban-American pilots and Argentine-born Guillermo Lares. Lares' brother Jorge Alberto was partially paralyzed Dec. 24 when his Brothers to the Rescue plane crashed because of an improperly installed fuel valve. At 8:30 A.M. on Thursday, Guillermo Lares led the pilots in a prayer next to one of the planes, asking for help finding boat people, for the fall of Fidel Castro and for his brother's recovery.

Each of the pilots was given a section of the Florida Straits to patrol—ranging over nearly 5,000 square miles among them. Brothers to the Rescue concentrates on the waters near Cuba, up to the territorial limit 12 miles from Cuba's coast, because boats that get close to Florida are more likely to make it and more likely to be discovered by American pleasure craft.

Each of the six Brothers to the Rescue planes bears a sticker for each raft it has found, the way fighter pilots mark their kills. To date, the organization has found 100 groups of boat people, according to Basulto, and 39 rafts, boats or inner tubes that were empty, floating in eloquent silence. "That's . . . that's . . . awful," said Mayte Greco, a Cuban-American woman who is one of the pilots. "You wonder, what if I'd gotten here 15 minutes earlier, or yesterday? You search a little bit," but it is fruitless.

On each flight, Brothers to the Rescue pilots report their presence to Cuban aviation authorities. Often they get no answer, but occasionally someone answers "good luck," according to Basulto. He said, "That is the purpose of this thing—we're trying to reach our people." His goal is to overthrow Castro.

Soviet Collapse Created Desperation

Cuban authorities publicly accuse Brothers to the Rescue of luring Cubans into the Straits by describing its rescues over Miami radio stations that can be heard in Cuba, and by welcoming rafters who make it to Florida as heroes. Basulto said he and other Cuban-Americans broadcast appeals not to take to rafts, but boat people ignore their warnings.

During 1991 and 1992, nearly 5,000 Cuban boat people arrived in Florida—a striking increase from years like 1990, when 467 came, or 1988, when there were only 59. Brothers to the Rescue began informally in 1990 and was incorporated as a non-profit organization in May 1991 in response to the sudden flood of boat people.

The exodus has coincided with the economic disaster that the Soviet Union's collapse brought on in Cuba, and it is not abating. So far this year 594 Cubans have arrived by sea.

It is illegal to enter the United States that way, but Cubans are automatically considered political refugees because their government is Communist, so they can stay and work here. No other people enjoy the same exemption, including those from other Communist countries. Haitians, for example, who pour into rickety vessels in even greater numbers than Cubans, are usually taken directly back to Haiti when found at sea.

Cubans can apply for visas to travel to the United States legally, but it can take years for the Cuban and American governments to grant permission.

Spotters Must Be Vigilant

At 9 A.M. Thursday four planes took off. Basulto's co-pilot was Steve Walton, an American Airlines pilot who said he had joined the group because "I hate totalitarian regimes and I really hate Communists."

A Brother to the Rescue "spotters guide" explains to visitors that they may talk inside the plane, but without looking at anyone. All eyes must search the water. "It only takes a moment to miss a raft adrift at sea," the pamphlet reads. After an hour of earnest staring, the waves began to look like innumerable mirages of boats, or monotonous wallpaper. To our own indignation, we began falling asleep.

Ricardo Ferro, the *St. Petersburg Times* photographer, said he felt guilty that one nod of his head might consign a boatload of people to drowning. We squirmed to keep awake and concentrate for another two hours.

At 11:55, Ferro suddenly shouted, "There! There! Right there!" The plane banked immediately to the right, where he pointed and in a few seconds we saw a thimble-sized white boat rocking on the waves, full of people stretching their arms into the air as if to grasp the plane.

We began circling the boat, swooping down several times to take a closer look. We thought we saw nine people, including one child who was lying on the floor of the boat, possibly too sick to move. Walton reported all of that to the U.S. Coast Guard. The boat was so near to Cuba that, circling 500 feet above it, we could easily see the island's coastline.

After a few minutes, we lost the boat and had to begin searching again. "Now I see how difficult it is to find them," Ferro said. We could see that the boat had an anchor out, and its motor was not running. It was evidently American, not Cuban, since it was in excellent shape and many of it occupants wore lifejackets, which are rare in Cuba.

Either some Cuban-Americans had made a dangerous and completely illegal trip into Cuba to spirit family or friends away from Cuba, or an American boat had picked up stranded rafters and then broken down itself, or the boat operators were smugglers who transport people for money. . . .

The Brothers to the Rescue planes circled the boat for 2½ hours, waiting for the Coast Guard. At 2:25 a bright orange HH 65 Dolphin helicopter arrived, flying low, and headed for the boat. Coast Guard Lt. Steve Newark, who flew in the helicopter, said later he had to seek special permission for the rescue because the boat was so close to Cuba.

Once permission was granted, the helicopter lowered a cage into the boat and slowly brought up seven people one by one. Four people, two Cubans and two Americans,

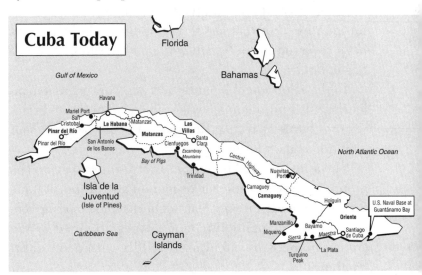

could not fit in the helicopter and were left behind.

Since the 23-foot boat was drifting toward Cuba, by the time the Coast Guard cutter *Shearwater* arrived to pick up the boat and its remaining four passengers, they were inside Cuban territorial waters, but the Coast Guard was able to act under the "right of assistance," or the right to rescue people in distress in any waters, according to Petty Officer Joe Dye, a Coast Guard spokesman.

A Cuban gunboat drew near and quietly observed the rescue.

Cubans Describe Deprivation

All 11 people were taken to Key West, interviewed by the Immigration and Naturalization Service and moved to the Transit Home for Cuban Refugees, a rented house in Key West. Set up in October [1992] to handle the increasing numbers of boat people, the house is run by Cuban-Americans, many of them former rafters.

"I have been waiting for that shower for years," said Lianet Monteagudo, 19, stepping out of it. She said shampoo, soap and toothpaste have become rare in Cuba. "I have not brushed my teeth (with toothpaste) for months— for months." For that last several months toothpaste has been reserved for pregnant women in her hometown of Sagua La Grande.

In the salon where Monteagudo was working as a manicurist, she said, shampoo was made from herbs and rainwater. A bottle of regular shampoo costs 230 pesos—about a month's salary for her.

She and Vivian Alamo, 27, another member of the group, unscrewed a stick of deodorant and peered at it before realizing what it was. Alamo's husband, showering separately and changing into new clothes provided by the transit home, sprayed himself wildly with deodorant, laughing.

Vivian Alamo said that in Cuba "desperation is so great there that people don't really care about anything," including the danger of dying on a trip from Cuba to Florida.

She said the eight friends who came together had been planning their trip since last October.

Asked for the details of how the eight Cubans came to be picked up by three Americans, the members of the group said they had been rescued after their own boat's motor failed.

Onelio Diaz, 28, another of the boat people, asked repeatedly that "El Pipa"—his nickname—be written down also. "Nobody in my hometown knows me by my real name," he said, "and in my house we don't have a radio, so when somebody hears the news, they might go tell my mother."

All arriving boat people's names are broadcast to Cuba over Miami's Spanish radio stations. Often families in Miami know from letters, coded phone messages, or notes carried by visitors from Cuba that their relatives are leaving by boat or raft.

Brothers to the Rescue and the Key West transit house get at least a half-dozen messages a day from anxious relatives in the United States and in Cuba. One wall of the transit house is covered with such messages. "Luis Delgado Gonzalez (19 years old), Ragnor Esteves Gonzalez (21 years old)," reads one of them. "They left the 17th of December, 1992 from Guanabo on a raft. Relative Rosa Mirada Gonzalez, aunt of Luis Delgado," and a phone number. Over the message, someone has written one word in large letters, "Muertos." Dead.

A Cuban American Woman's Reflections

Liz Balmaseda

Although she came to Miami as an infant, Liz Balmaseda grew up arguably more Cuban than American. In the following selection, Balmaseda reflects on her life as a Cuban American, exploring the culture that she and her fellow Cuban immigrants so fiercely protect. Like many Cuban Americans, she wonders about the future, when Fidel Castro will no longer be in power. She also discusses extremism and isolationism within the exile community. The author is a columnist for the *Miami Herald*. She won a Pulitzer Prize in 1992 for her series of commentaries about Cuban Americans in Miami.

It is, at its most luminous stretch, a reflection. In its lights and arches, in its shrines and labyrinths, in its exuberance and anguish, it is a reflection. Havana twinkles in Miami, its music echoes along the streets of exile, its spirit moves throughout the parlors of the elite, the kitchens of the working class.

It is always there: Cuba. Nothing has been sufficiently powerful to erase its presence or to co-opt the culture. Like the salty air from the sea that connects the island and the diaspora, it is there. In four decades of exodus and exile, this transported spirit of Cuba has risen in a complex city, my city. When I was growing up in Hialeah, the sprawling industrial city just north of Miami that later came to be known as *La ciudad que progresa* [city that progresses], I could see Cuba all over the place. I could find Cuba even on Thanksgiving Day, the most American of holidays, in the *frijoles negros* [black beans] that steamed next to the perfect foreign cylinder of cranberry jelly. But it existed only in the most poetic terms. It was a place where the palm tree trunks were whiter, more beautiful even than the soaring royal palm trees that stood guard at the Hialeah racetrack. It was a place where the beaches were lovelier, better than any beach along any old Miami strip. The sugar was sweeter, the air cleaner, the seashells more stunning. Cuba was so breathtaking, and its absence so devastating, that everyone would cry when the Cuban National Anthem was played at the *Añorada Cuba Show*[1] each year. Even I, who had landed in Miami as an infant, who could not remember the palm trees or the sugar, who could not describe the seaside band shell in my native Puerto Padre, who did not even know the words to the Cuban National Anthem, cried, too. Cuba was that big.

Dreaming of Cuba

I grew up believing Cuba was a place that existed only in black and white and exact shades of gray. It was as if all of my relatives on the island existed in another dimension, a kind of grainy freeze-frame. It was one giant prison, Cuba. Its black and white brutality—what kind of place would forbid my mother's parents from coming to Miami?—contrasted sharply with the colors and sounds of my world. My world was full of rumba and reds, passionate debates about communism, and frequent exhortations to fight for *libertad* [liberty]. And all this thunder for Cuba resounded against a larger landscape of American pop culture.

1. annual musical show dedicated to promoting the continuation of Cuban culture in exile

I came to believe no other immigrant population in this country has been more scrutinized, analyzed, and less homogenized than Cuban Miami. Perhaps that is because ours is not an immigrant community. It has been called a true enclave. It is often said, with some exaggeration, that one can live and die in Cuban Miami without speaking a word of English. Perhaps that is an oversimplification, but it serves to illustrate a rare independence and a certain detachment from other Latino communities.

Our particular identity has been that we are exiles. At the risk of isolation from the streams of assimilation, we are *el exilio*, a banner that has brought on charges of arrogance and the wrath of the white flight stragglers. Not immigrants or émigrés or refugees, not documented or undocumented, we are exiles in a city built on nostalgia.

Obsessed with Castro

In our decades-old scramble not to forget, we have raised shrines, named streets, erected monuments, attempted replicas from memory and sepia prints. And stroke by stroke a landscape has taken shape, defined by streets named Ronald Reagan and Celia Cruz and *Añorada Cuba* (Cuba of My Yearning) Way, a park where old Cuban men play dominoes, a bayside shrine where recent refugees come to leave scraps of their rafts in gratitude at the feet of a *café-con-leche*—colored Virgin, a supermarket named Varadero. It is also defined by political riptides, an artistic and cultural renaissance, the identity struggles of the second generation, a language native to exile, pride, nostalgia, pain. It is deceivingly familiar, this place of royal palms and tropical fruit stands and Cuban flamingos and Cuban tile. It is not Cuba.

Just like Havana, Miami is Castrocentric. More than Republican or Democrat, black or white, male or female, Cuban Miami has revolved around the doings and undoings of Fidel Castro. For three and one-half decades he has been the axis upon which all good and evil, rage and reason, fact and fiction spin.

Just as it has kept the torch lit for the fatherland, the Castro obsession is also what has spawned Cuban Miami's darker side, the incidents of terrorism, the bouts of intolerance, the strong-arm power-brokering in the name of anti-Communism, the banning of musicians and writers and artists who are somehow identified with the Castro regime.

In consequence, an image of exile Miami as a knee-jerk, reactionary monolith has been hard to shake, even though the reality is different, a pluralistic, diverse community that is too often marred by a narrow extremist streak: There are working class parents who raise sons and daughters to be architects, developers, doctors, and lawyers; former Havana socialites who have been forced by the equalizing nature of exile to commingle in their elderly years with poor sugar mill workers and farmers; *batistianos* [followers of Fulgencio Batista] and the *fidelistas* [followers of Castro]; ex–political prisoners and celebrities; people who watched decades of their lives evaporate inside repressive, dank, Cuban prisons and their American children, grandchildren, and great-grandchildren. Luminaries of Castro's bohemian brat pack paint and write and ruminate in Miami. Yesterday's revolutionaries are today's checkout clerks. There are the young, identity-obsessed and often consumed by recapturing the long ago and far away, while nostalgia-bound older generations yearn for what once was.

Growing Up Cuban American

I grew up thinking I was Cuban. It was why my mom wouldn't let me stay for sleepovers with the other Girl Scouts in my troop. It was why I was the only one in my troop who put sugar in hot chocolate. It must be because

I'm Cuban, I used to think growing up in Hialeah. Cubans put sugar in everything. We even used to put it on top of buttered crackers. None of my American friends did that. They never sliced bananas into their red bean puree—well, they didn't even have red bean puree.

I was Cuban because I was different from the *americanito* kids in elementary school. They never seemed to have parties at their houses or any cousins. I had a ton of cousins because I was Cuban. Ours was a wounded population, and the wounds often have imposed an invisible structure, guiding political agendas, barring forgiveness, fanning intransigence.

Sometimes, life in Cuban Miami has too often seemed to be what we have while we don't have Cuba. At times it can be described as simply as absence of revolution. Yet, in this exile waiting room pulses a whole new history, a new culture amid the trappings of American life: government contracts, Miami Dolphin football games, real estate deals, marriages, graduations, happy hour, a deceiving air of assimilation.

Underneath it all, there is Cuba. It turns up as a bizarre foreign policy allusion in city commissioner races, as patriotic decor in car dealerships, in commercial jingles. We've created a new kind of hybrid culture between the magnified Havana of our memories and our dreams and the changed Miami of our reality. This is not merely a story of waiting. The impact of the exile presence has been enormous, politically, economically, culturally.

There are Cubans in Congress, in the state legislature, in the president's and vice-president's offices at colleges and universities, in the CEO's inner sanctum. We know the list: Gloria Estefan, Andy García, the late president of Coca Cola, Oscar Hijuelos. We have won Grammies, Emmies, genius grants. Our deeds have triggered important debates, not only about political action or U.S. foreign policy, but also about immigration and language. And our success and our image as entrenched and hermetically sealed in our culture, has set off a backlash; but it hasn't detained the momentum.

Questions About the Future

With every migration, the flame of the *cubania* is rekindled; the conjured Havana is made fresh once again. The flame often fuels an intense limbo. There have been great strides in and out of the community. But there also have been failures: mud trekked in the Everglades by weekend commandos on futile missions, hot air that rarely leaves the confines of Little Havana. From the outside, the image is usually of the ferocious exiles who think the same, blinded by their anti-castrismo. But who are we?

We are a population so deeply rooted in Miami we seem entrenched in the city's character. Yet, and this is the great irony, we are a people who, in a flash, had to leave our mothers and fathers, children, sisters, and brothers and start all over again. We are daughters and sons who said good-bye, see you next week, and then didn't see their parents again for 25 years.

I think the better questions are these: What will there be once Fidel falls? What will there be in Cuba? What will there be in Miami? We will be exile no more, simply the protagonists of a particular capsule in time, a village of tiny lights, distant but no longer displaced.

Elian Gonzalez: A Young Refugee Polarizes the Cuban American Community

Margaret D. Wilde

The exodus of raft and boat people fleeing hardship in Cuba continued throughout the 1990s. Five-year-old Elian Gonzalez was plucked from the sea by American fishermen after his boat overturned and his mother drowned. After a brief hospital stay, Elian was sent to relatives in Miami, who were adamant that he should stay in the United States. Elian was ultimately removed from the home during a federal raid and returned to his father in Cuba. In the following selection, Margaret D. Wilde discusses how the debate over Elian's fate polarized Cuban Americans in Miami but also planted the seeds for dialogue within the exile community. Wilde is a former editor at large for *Christian Century* magazine.

The camera panned away from a garbage fire in the middle of the street and followed the young men who had set it. The men were calling to a nearby band of demonstrators. "The people are afraid they might be provocateurs, under orders from Castro," said the television announcer. "This is rowdier than most Miami traffic jams, but it isn't a riot; it's the beginning of a catharsis."

Margaret D. Wilde, "Cuban American Dialogues," *Christian Century*, May 17, 2000, p. 556. Copyright © 2000 by The Christian Century Foundation. Reproduced by permission.

The disturbances that followed the removal of Elian Gonzalez from his Miami relatives' home by armed federal agents ware indeed part of a catharsis, though not its beginning. The outpouring of emotion started months earlier, not on the streets but in homes and churches, away from the television cameras. Some people say they are angrier than they've been in years, but they are also talking and listening to each other more. If that continues, there is hope for dialogue within the Cuban exile community—which is probably prerequisite for dialogue with the rest of the city.

Political Discussion Is Rare

Of the more than 700,000 Cuban-Americans in metropolitan Miami, perhaps a third identify with the fervent anti-Castro old guard. At the other extreme, a small group (mostly younger and American-educated) favor normalizing political and economic relations with Cuba, although they remain critical of the Castro regime. In between are what some call the "silent majority," who visit or send money and material aid to friends and relatives on the island, but avoid confrontation with the old guard.

There is little public discussion among these groups. "We don't talk about dialogue," says Quaker peace advocate Eduardo Diaz. "Dialoguero has been a fighting word since the 1970s," he says, for it was a term applied to those who supported negotiations with Castro. Others point out that public disagreement was never an option for ordinary citizens in Cuba, and for Miami Cubans it seems disloyal—"like hanging out our underwear for everyone to see."

Families have their own ways of communicating across the divide. "We know everyone's viewpoint without making them say it," a college student told me. "By the end of dinner we all understand each other, and no one goes away angry."

I once heard two sisters talking about how they had persuaded their father to help pay for an expensive prescription that his brother in Cuba had asked for. "It was scary; I thought he would choke on his meat," said one sister. "He knew all along that we were sending Uncle money," the other reassured her. "It was hard this time because we couldn't do it alone, but you watch: next week he'll be asking how Uncle is doing."

Elian Gonzalez Sparks Debate

With Elian [Gonzalez] it was hard to separate the language of politics from the language of the heart. At first he was a safe subject of conversation: an innocent, five-year-old child, plucked from the sea in a miraculous [1999] Thanksgiving Day rescue. Of course he would stay, and his father would find a way to join him; how could the immigration agents gainsay a miracle? But when Juan Miguel Gonzalez said he wanted his son back in Cuba, the conversation suddenly became complicated.

To deny the father's right meant overriding the cherished principle of patria potestad—parental or, more literally, paternal authority. For some exile leaders, that was easy to do, since they were struck by the irony of Juan Miguel invoking a right that in Cuba is routinely usurped by the government. But many people were still reluctant to abandon the principle. Said a Cuban-born priest: "You can see how much we care about Elian, if we're willing to go against patria potestad to save him."

Beneath this debate lay devastating memories of family separation. Some 14,000 Cuban children were sent away by their parents in the 1960s on a church-sponsored airlift called Operation Pedro Pan. Others were torn away from loved ones by Cuban officials, never to hear from them again; or by the raging sea, as Elian's mother was. Elian has been a reminder of how divided Cuban families are. It is too painful to talk about, and too important not to.

Lessons of History Are Revisited

He has also forced the Cuban community to acknowledge its own unspoken political divisions. Most people agree that the old guard is losing numbers and energy. "The young have no memory," one said ruefully on a radio talk show. "And they don't learn their own history in American schools, only tolerance and political relativism." Perhaps Elian is changing that, said another. "Young people, children—even the imbeciles who talk about ending the embargo—they're all coming out [to demonstrations at the Gonzalez home], and seeing why we care so much. They're learning about their past, lessons they never got in school."

Those lessons include a litany of perceived betrayals by the U.S. government: the Bay of Pigs invasion in 1961, the Cuban missile crisis in 1962, the post-Mariel agreement to halt the flow of refugees in 1980, the downing of the Brothers to the Rescue plane in 1996. Now [in 2000] President [Bill] Clinton hopes to normalize relations with Cuba in order to expedite trade agreements. It is already a done deal, many exiles said: Clinton would sacrifice an innocent child for the sake of the new world economic order.

"Folks are suffering right now," says Eduardo Diaz. "Elian reminds them of all the impotence they've ever experienced." Peacemakers call this unresolved anger and mourning, and they know that the appropriate response is to listen to people—without judging, offering reality checks, or pressuring them into dialogue.

Non-Cuban Americans Have Different Opinions

That has not been the response of the Cuban exiles' American neighbors. A *Miami Herald* poll in early April [2000] showed that 76 percent of white, non-Hispanic Miamians and 92 percent of African-Americans favored Elian's repatriation to Cuba with his father, compared to 9 percent of

Cubans. The survey director said that in 20 years of polling in Miami, he had never seen results that set Cubans and the other two groups so far apart. A week later, political analyst Max Castro admonished his fellow exiles: "When, after 40 years of preaching the cause, your neighbors in your community are the least convinced people in the world, it's time for a reality check and not just better public relations."

Liz Balmaseda, another Cuban-born columnist, reflects a more widespread view. She sees indifference to the Cuban cause as "simply another surfacing of America's anti-immigrant undertow," especially against the exile community with "its Miami-generated political clout." The public, she says, "doesn't hear the rest of the story. It doesn't hear about the refugee parents whose children are still stuck in Cuba because the Fidel Castro government refuses them exit permits. . . . It doesn't hear about the would-be rafters who are jailed for simply trying to leave the island." Instead, the press has reduced "our enormously painful history to a few clever, recyclable phrases."

A woman in front of the Gonzalez home wasn't blaming the press. She shook her head sadly as people shouted slogans into a reporter's microphone. "I agree with what they're saying; that's why I'm here," she said. "But I would say it differently."

"Then why don't you?" a man near us snapped at her. "Who stole your tongue?" "People like that," she said, turning away from him. "They do all the talking. We don't even try any more."

New Forms of Protest Emerge

The struggle over Elian has produced two new forms of political protest, however: a human chain, which was well practiced but could not form in time to stop the sudden, early-morning raid, and a "rolling blockade" of cars driving slowly on major thoroughfares. The rolling blockade was harder to defeat than the human chain, but it also produced more backlash. Cuban-American leaders likened it to the Montgomery bus boycott, but many African-Americans called the comparison a mockery of the civil rights movement—and commuters called it economic strangulation. "Civil disobedience doesn't come easily to us," said one blockade driver. "We haven't seen it work, and we're afraid of making more enemies. But it was new at first to black people too, and they learned; so can we."

Some liberals and moderates distrust the Democracia Movement, which organized both actions. Until now, the group was best known for sailing sport-fishing boats with banners into Cuban waters, a potentially provocative tactic; and its leader, Ramon Saul Sanchez, was once associated with violent anti-Castro groups. "It looks like the old guard in sheep's clothing," a liberal activist told me. "But I'd like to be proven wrong. If they are still teaching nonviolence after the Elian battle is over, I'll be a believer too. A lot of people will."

"Dios te salve Maria, llena eres de gracia" [Hail Mary, full of grace]. Besides political slogans, prayer was the most common language in the struggle for Elian. Outside the Gonzalez home, Catholics distributed rosaries and led the Hail Mary; a few yards away, shouts of "Aleluia!" and "Amen, Senor!" bespoke a strong evangelical presence. Catholic and Protestant clergy took turns at a makeshift pulpit every evening, and on Friday they led worship together. "Each of us is willing to sacrifice," Francisco Santana, the family's priest, told a *Herald* reporter. "When we have a service in common we avoid mentioning the things that divide us, like the devotion to Mary, and we center ourselves in our faith in the Lord Jesus."

In contrast to the fervent advocacy of some Cuban-American clergy, the Catholic archdiocese and most Protestant leaders tried to maintain neutrality. Auxiliary

Bishop Agustin Roman, who has publicly intervened in other crises, said that the Catholic Church must work with the whole Gonzalez family. Protestant pastors felt "caught in the middle," one of them told me. "There are many Cubans in our congregations, and also many Americans who strongly support the father. We were really embarrassed by the National Council of Churches' taking sides with the father."

The district office of the United Methodist Church was also embarrassed when an agency of the church set up a fund for voluntary contributions toward the father's legal expenses. It was unfortunate, superintendent Clark Campbell-Evans told me later, that the denomination "took action without first coming here to listen; that was the wrong way to proceed." He said the Cuban-American reality is "vital to us as a community of faith; we have to learn to hear and honor their stories." United Methodist officials have since promised to come for a Miami meeting, Campbell-Evans said.

A Plan to Heal the Wounds

On Easter Sunday, Miami officials, who were under heavy criticism for allowing police participation in the federal raid the day before, announced plans for a Miami-Dade Mosaic initiative, led by "dozens of ethnic, civic and religious leaders and economic empowerment agencies." Robert Simms, a former director of the Community Relations Board, said that, based on experience with the African-American community, successful discussion requires leaders in the grieving community "to step forward and articulate the concerns of those who are offended. . . . You let people vent. Then you bring in leaders who can transfer pain into an action plan."

The plan promises wide participation rather than a blue-ribbon panel, but it may not work as quickly as city leaders hope. There are differences between this crisis and the ones caused by African-American grievances in recent years. By the 1980s, after long experience in the civil rights movement, the black community had strong leaders and a relatively unified vision. Cuban-Americans are more polarized and less comfortable with public dialogue. And while African-Americans were slowly making their grievances heard, Cuban-Americans were becoming convinced that no one would listen to them. It may take time to reverse that distrust.

Most non-Cubans see Elian's story as a private tragedy turned into a political football by opportunistic politicians; Cuban-Americans see him as a symbol of their own private tragedies, which are in fact political. "We're all footballs," said one. "If you haven't been kicked around as we have, by both Washington and Havana, you won't understand."

After 41 years in which a few Cuban-Americans have done most of the talking, the Cuban community shouldn't be rushed into an "action plan." It needs time for more venting and dialogue.

Cuban Families Adapt to American Life

Thomas D. Boswell and James R. Curtis

As in all immigrant communities, Cuban American families face challenges in retaining their cultural identity while
assimilating into their new country. In this selection,
Thomas D. Boswell and James R. Curtis explore the difficulties of second-generation Cuban Americans who have
gradually become more American than Cuban. The authors
conclude that assimilation inevitably creates friction within
immigrant families. Thomas Boswell is a professor of geol-
ogy at the University of Miami; James Curtis is a professor
of geography at California State University, Long Beach.

Change is a central and unavoidable aspect of the immigrant experience in America. Initially, the acceptance of
American ways may be resisted, especially among the first
generation immigrants clinging to familiar and comfortable cultural patterns of their homeland. For them, the
new culture is unknown and often suspect. Yet in spite of
the most diligent and self-conscious efforts of immigrant
groups to preserve their heritage, changes inevitably occur.
The dynamics of acculturation and assimilation, however,
proceed differentially; some elements (such as language
and adornment) tend to vanish quickly, whereas others
(such as religion and cuisine) may persist for generations,
perhaps even indefinitely. Typically the pace of change ac-
celerates along generational lines as rates of out-marriage,

movement from traditional ethnic enclaves and, of course, acceptance of the ways of the host culture increase.

Although these changes are institutional and exist at a group level, they are also personal. Perhaps most immediately and intimately, they are felt in the home and among the youth. In this context, it is often the family that suffers the brunt of conflict between the new and the old cultures. The accepted structure of the family and the role of its members may be questioned and ultimately re-aligned. This, clearly, is the case among Cuban-Americans. . . .

The Cuban-American Family

Generally speaking, the family has played a somewhat different role in traditional Cuban society than it has in the United States. Prior to 1959, a Cuban's self-confidence, sense of security, and identity were established primarily through family relationships. In contrast to the individulalism of the United States, which values an individual in terms of his or her abilities to compete independently for socioeconomic status, the culture of Cuba viewed life as a network of personal relationships. The Cuban relies and trusts persons; he or she knows that in times of trouble a close friend or relative can be counted upon for needed assistance. A Cuban relies less on impersonal secondary relationships and generally does not trust or place much faith in large organizations. At least this was the case in Cuba prior to Castro's revolution. Such an attitude is not unique to Cuba but rather is typical of most Latin American societies.

One way in which the greater emphasis that is placed on the Cuban family can be illustrated is through its use of surnames. English custom in United States society dictates that family names be derived patrilinealy. In Latin American societies it is more common for a person to have two surnames, representing both the father's and mother's sides of the family. For instance, a man with the name of Ricardo Gomez Gonzales had his name derived in the following way. His given name is Ricardo and his two surnames are Gomez and Gonzales. Gomez was his father's family name and Gonzales was his mother's family name. Suppose that a woman by the name of Maria Garcia Rivera married Mr. Gomez. Her new name would become Maria Garcia de Gomez. She would retain her father's surname, drop her mother's name, and add her husband's father's name after the "de." In fact, for formal occasions, even more complicated combinations of names frequently are used. To avoid confusion, many Cuban-Americans have adopted the American custom of using only the surname of the father.

Another characteristic of traditional Cuban society that illustrated a reliance on personal relationships is the institution known as *compadrazgo*. It is somewhat similar to the tradition of godparents in the United States, except that it is usually taken more seriously by Cubans and often involves a higher level of personal obligation. Under the *compadrazgo* system a set of *compadres* are selected for each child. These are best thought of as being "companion parents" with the child's natural parents. Sometimes they are selected when the parents are married, but they might be decided upon at the time of the child's baptism or perhaps confirmation. The *compadres* are sometimes relatives, but often they are not. But if they are not blood relatives, they become de facto members of the family upon becoming *compadres*. The purpose of a *compadre* is to offer both economic and moral assistance to the family whenever it is needed. He or she may feel freer to give advice in regard to family problems than a brother or sister of the father or mother would. It is essential that *compadres* live close to the family they are associated with, so that frequent contact can be made and the necessary obligations honored.

Roles Are Changing

In the traditional Cuban family there was a sharp distinction between the role of men and women, with a double standard being applied in work, play, and sex. The wife was expected to stay at home and attend to the running of the household and care for the children. A pattern of male-dominance prevailed, where most of the major family decisions were made by the husband. The tradition of *machismo* dictated that males demonstrate virility through physical strength, courage, and business success. It was common, and considered proper, for males to have extramarital affairs. Whether or not a husband had a regular mistress was frequently more affected by economics than conscience. Daughters and wives were to be protected against temptation. A strict tradition of chaperoning was in effect for respectable, unmarried women who dated.

Sociologists have developed a concept known as *resource theory* for explaining the position of decision-making power that the members of any particular family have relative to each other. An individual gains in power if the resources that he or she contributes to the family increases. These resources may be economic, intellectual, or emotional. One of the important circumstances that affected the adjustment of Cuban immigrants was the economic difficulties that many faced upon their arrival in the United States. Often, the husband would be unable to find work, or would find work at a lower status level than he had experienced in Cuba. As a result, it became necessary for many wives to enter the labor force to help contribute to the support of the family. In 1980 slightly over half of all women over 16 years of age of Cuban descent in the United States were in the labor force. A survey of women in West New York found that less than one-fourth worked in Cuba before coming to the United States. And as the wife's resource contribution to the family became greater through her employment, usually her power to make decisions also increased, while that of her husband declined. A recent study of Cuban women in Washington, D.C., concludes that their entrance into the labor force is the single most important change in their lives as immigrants. As a result, the traditional patriarchal family structure for Cuban-Americans began to change toward greater equality in decision-making abilities for husbands and wives. Length of residence in the United States and degree of association with Americans were also positively associated with level of equality or independence within the family. As a result, Cuban-American families are less male dominated and the roles of husbands and wives are less segregated than the traditional Latin American family norm that typified Cuba before 1959.

Caught Between Cultures

Despite the fact that Cuban family structure has changed in the United States, it is still different enough from the American norm to cause some conflict between first- and second-generation Cuban-Americans. Studies of acculturation stresses among Cubans living in the United States have found that the second generation, which was the first born in America, generally adopts Anglo attitudes and behavior patterns more quickly than their parents. Sometimes a crisis in authority emerges, as the parents find themselves being led and instructed in new ways by their children. Many of the traditional norms of the Cuban family became labeled old-fashioned. Chaperoning for dating, for example, has become a focal point of tension in many families. Many second-generation Cuban-Americans feel they are caught between two cultures, being neither completely Cuban nor American. They want to maintain selected aspects of both cultures, and as a result feel that they do not belong to (or are not completely accepted by) either.

Another aspect of the Cuban-American family that distinguishes it from the contemporary American family is the tendency for Cuban households to include relatives in the nuclear family. The U.S. Census Bureau indicates that about 9 percent of all persons of Cuban descent live in households where there are "other relatives" (other than wife or child) of the head of the household. The corresponding figure for all persons of Spanish origin is about 6 percent, while for the non-Spanish it is approximately 4 percent. Often this additional relative is a widowed and dependent grandparent, who came to the United States after the nuclear family arrived. Because so many Cuban-American women work, the elderly became important as housekeepers and babysitters and for passing on the culture and language to the new-generation children.

Marriage Customs Change

One important factor that is having an impact on the survival of the traditional Cuban family in the United States is the high out-marriage rate of Cuban-Americans. For 1970, 17 percent of all women of Cuban descent had married non-Cubans. However, many of the marriages to Cubans took place in Cuba before arrival in the United States. When only second-generation, American-born women are considered, it was found that 46 percent of those married had married non-Spanish husbands. The comparable figures for women of Puerto Rican and Mexican descent were 33 and 16 percent, respectively. Second-generation Cubans have exhibited an extraordinarily high rate of out-marriage, which would appear to indicate a very rapid tendency toward assimilation. A recent comparative study of out-marriage patterns of Hispanic groups living in New York City determined that Cubans had the highest out-group marriage rates. It also found that the degree of out-marriage is much higher among second-generation,

American-born children than for their foreign-born Hispanic parents. In addition, persons with higher socioeconomic status, those who were older at the time they married, and those who had been married more than once, all showed higher out-marriage rates. The relative degree of spatial concentration proved to be the strongest determinant of exogamous marriage rates. Groups that were more dispersed residentially throughout New York City exhibited higher out-marriage rates. The rate of intergroup marriage was also considerably higher for Cubans living in New York than for those living in New Jersey and Florida, possibly because more Cubans live in New Jersey and Florida.

It is clear that most of the Cubans who immigrated to the United States have carried with them the tradition of the Cuban family. This tradition emphasizes personal relationships, the use of both maternal and paternal family names, the institution of *compadrazgo*, and a double standard for male and female behavior. However, the longer the period of residence in the United States the more this tradition erodes. For instance, most second-generation Cuban-Americans seldom use their maternal surnames, the significance of *compadres* has become diluted, the sexual double standard is weakening, and out-marriage is becoming very common. Nevertheless, despite these changes, the typical Cuban-American family is still significantly different from the typical United States family norm. . . .

The 1980 census (which was taken before the massive Mariel exodus) revealed that 40.6 percent of the total Cuban-American population was below the age of 25. In Dade County alone it is estimated that there are over 225,000 Cubans in this age group. Although a majority were born in Cuba, most left the island at an early age; Cuba is often just a vague memory for them. Many others, of course, were born in this country. For these Cuban youths, most or all of their lives have been spent in the

United States and they have been duly influenced by American values and institutions. Yet at the same time their Cuban heritage is typically instilled by strong familial ties and a social system that places great value in the preservation of Cuban culture in the United States. Consequently, they are the products of two cultures. In this sense, they form a new subcultural group unique in its mixture of elements drawn from the two traditions.

There are, of course, potential advantages as well as liabilities that young Cuban-Americans face in this position between two cultures. Ideally, it affords them the opportunity of capitalizing on the best features of each group and of establishing an extended social network that bridges the gap between the two. Some Cuban youths, in fact, have shaped a pattern of existence in which they feel equally comfortable in either setting and enjoy the differences. In order to accomplish this transition they must have command of both languages. Their bilingual skills and familiarity with the two cultures also greatly enhance their employment opportunities, especially in Miami.

At the opposite extreme, for a number of young Cuban-Americans this situation has led to an identity crisis; they do not feel completely Cuban or American. This has led a few to Anglicize their names, either informally or officially, in order to feel more American. Some lack sufficient development in either Spanish or English to function effectively and without fear of embarrassment in more formal settings in either culture. For these young people, their economic opportunities and lifestyle alternatives may be severely restricted. It is not unusual for them to limit their voluntary social interactions to fellow young Cubans who share similar circumstances. Because of its large concentration of Cuban-American youths, Miami may be the only place where some young Cubans raised in south Florida feel a sense of belonging and a measure of security in numbers.

Individual rates of adjustment for young Cuban-Americans vary widely between the two extremes suggested above. It is probably true that all face a certain amount of conflict resolution between the often opposing values and traditions of their Cuban heritage and the American society in which they live. In most cases, concessions are made to both cultures. Double-role-playing is also common. At home, for example, they may "act" more Cuban than at school or with friends in which they "act" more American. The degree to which either Cuban or American elements are stressed tends to vary as well by age or life stage. During the early and middle teenage years, for instance, American ways are often emphasized. This is largely a consequence of peer group pressure and an emerging sense of independence. At marriage and especially at the stage of early parenthood, however, there is frequently a reaffirmation of their Cuban heritage as they begin to consider the values they wish to pass on to their children.

Clinging to Tradition

Some of the established Cuban traditions that have generated considerable conflict in the past between Cuban-American parents and children are gradually changing. The custom of a chaperon (usually a parent or older relative) accompanying unmarried couples on dates is one example. Although chaperons are still part of the social scene for a vast majority of younger teenagers, many parents now allow older teenagers and young adults to go on dates alone; group functions and double dating, however, are strongly encouraged. Other customs have not changed as quickly, especially regarding girls and young women, who tend to be extremely protected by their families. Unmarried females are still expected to live at home until they marry, even if they work and could afford to move into their own house or apartment. It has been suggested that this is one reason why a higher percentage of Cuban-American female college students attend schools in or near their hometowns than do their male counterparts.

Cuban-American youth have fashioned a distinctive lifestyle that freely incorporates elements of both cultures. In some cases these elements are mixed together to create a synthesis that is unique and somewhat particular to the place in which the fusion occurs. It is a dynamic lifestyle that is continually in flux and evolving in response to new influences and shifts in popular culture. It also serves an important social function for many young people in the Cuban-American community by fostering a sense of subcultural identity.

Language is the most obvious area where this process has occurred. Spanish and English words and phrases are mixed and jumbled together to form a new linguistic synthesis that has been popularly labeled "Spanglish." For perhaps a majority of Cuban-American youths it is the language they feel most comfortable speaking, at least among themselves. Yet while Spanish may be spoken at home and Spanglish when with Cuban friends, English-language movies and television programs are preferred over those in Spanish.

Culture Has Crossover Appeal

Music is another cultural element that has tremendous crossover appeal. Most Cuban-American young people have been thoroughly exposed to and appreciate both Latin and American music. They may listen to radio stations that play American rock or jazz or country and western, and then turn the dial to a Spanish language station and catch the latest *salsa* sounds. Some of the Spanish radio stations in Miami aimed at a younger audience, such as WQTU-FM ("Super Q"), incorporate popular American rock tunes into their program. The two musical traditions are also commonly fused, giving rise to new musical expressions. A number of popular young Cuban-American groups in Miami, such as the Miami Sound Machine, Alma, and Clouds, have enjoyed commercial success in recent years by blending contemporary Latin and American musical styles.

A host of other cultural elements from both traditions are likewise mixed. On the dance floor, for example, they may perform the latest disco dance on one occasion, and then on another dance the *rumba* or *chachachá*. Traditional Cuban food is generally served and enjoyed at home, but when dining out they prefer to go to an American fast-food restaurant and have the standard order of hamburgers, french fries, and a Coke. And while many Cuban-American girls and young women may prefer to wear the latest fashion in jeans, their mothers may insist that the jeans be tailored and pressed to avoid a casual appearance, which many Cuban parents consider to be inappropriate.

In certain instances, the results of these mixtures have been criticized by some Cuban-Americans, including young people, as representing the worst of both cultures. One phenomenon that has drawn criticism by many is the *Fiesta de Quince Anos*. On a Cuban girl's fifteenth birthday, it is customary to commemorate the occasion by giving a party. It is similar to a "coming out" or debutante celebration, and traditionally marked the age when girls were considered marriageable, or more recently, allowed to increase their social activities, including dating. In Cuba, the wealthy typically held *quince* parties at social clubs; *quinces* for the working class were more family-oriented and generally took place at home. In the United States, especially in Miami, they have become a major social event for many middle-class Cubans. The parties have grown conspicuously in size and expense. It is not unusual for some families to spend thousands of dollars on the party, which may necessitate a "quince loan." In some cases, the parties have

evolved into such big affairs that they would be more ap-
propriately classified as extravaganzas, even spectacles, that
attempt to exceed each other in grandeur and consumption.
One father, for example, rented the Orange Bowl for his
daughter's *quince!* Girls have arrived at their parties in
horse-drawn carriages, in helicopters, and in simulated
rockets, while others have popped out of cakes and emerged
from bird-cages. A humor columnist for *El Herald,* George
Childs, wrote about his vision of the ultimate *quince:* a girl
is fired out of a cannon two blocks away, lands in a specially
created fountain, while the Goodyear blimp drops 15 boys
dressed as Robin Hood and 15 girls float down in Cleopatra costumes. *Quince* celebrations have been used by some
Cuban-Americans as a symbol of the success they have attained in the United States, one way of showing their financial well being. But they have been criticized as examples of American commercialization and materialism
misapplied to an important Cuban tradition that could seriously damage its original meaning. . . .

Where Do Cuban-Americans Fit?

The Cuban-Americans have made remarkable progress in
their adjustment to life in the United States. . . . The first
immigrants to arrive from Cuba after the Castro takeover
in 1959 were above average in terms of their educational
background and entrepreneurial skills. As happened with
most other ethnic groups, these first arrivals were able to
establish an economic and cultural base that would ease
the difficulties of adjustment for later waves of Cuban
refugees, who were not so wealthy or skilled. The Cubans
who chose not to locate in the ethnic enclaves of Miami
and Union City–West New York settled mainly in other
large cities where they received considerable government
assistance under the Cuban Refugee Program.

By almost any measure it is clear that Cubans are becoming rapidly assimilated into American society, although they still are readily visible as an ethnic minority. Most of the first-generation immigrants from Cuba and their second-generation American-born children are well on the way toward social or structural assimilation. . . .

Most Cuban-Americans have given up the hope and desire of returning to Cuba, even if Castro were to be overthrown by a democratic regime. As a result, most either have (or would like to have) United States citizenship status. Those who possess citizenship exhibit high levels of participation in the American electoral process. Politically, they have become very well integrated into the American system. The increasing desire for United States citizenship is an indication that these individuals are identifying themselves more as Americans and less as Cubans. This tendency provides further evidence of social assimilation. . . .

In terms of language, Cuban assimilation appears to be occurring primarily along generational lines. That is, the second- and third-generation Cuban-Americans have developed the greatest facility with English. A recent study conducted by a University of Florida linguistic anthropologist determined that Cubans are learning English as fast or faster than any other group of immigrants in United States history. Typically, the second generation is bilingual, while the third usually is fluent only in English. Although the first generation is more comfortable when speaking Spanish, an increasing percentage is learning English. Still, their difficulty with understanding English is usually considered to be one of the most severe problems they have had to face while living in the United States. Nevertheless, there is an unmistakable drift toward the use of English and away from the use of Spanish as the generations increase.

CHAPTER 4

The Accomplishments of Cuban Americans

COMING TO AMERICA

Desi Arnaz: Rising to Stardom

Warren G. Harris

Desi Arnaz III was born into a life of wealth and privilege in Cuba. His father, Desi Arnaz II, was the mayor of Santiago and loyal to the political regime of Gerardo Machado. In 1933, Machado was forced out of office and into exile in the United States. The same year, Fulgencio Batista, who assumed power in a military coup, insisted that Machado's remaining supporters, including Desi Arnaz II, leave the island. When young Desi Arnaz joined his exiled father in Miami in 1934, he experienced poverty for the first time. In the following excerpt, author Warren G. Harris describes how Arnaz struggled to get by and how his natural talents quickly led him into show business, where he soon became the leader of his own Latin band. Harris shows how even in the early days of Arnaz's career, before he costarred with his wife, Lucille Ball, in the television comedy *I Love Lucy*, Arnaz's musical talent and showmanship made him a star in his own right. Harris has written biographies of numerous Hollywood celebrities.

In June 1934, seventeen-year-old Desi [Arnaz] stepped off the ferry at Key West and into his father's arms. "When they let me through immigration, I gave Dad the longest, biggest, and tightest *abrazo* [hug] ever. He said, '*Bienvenido a Los Estados Unidos de Norte America*,[1] and those

1. Spanish for "Welcome to the United States of North America"

will be the last Spanish words I will speak to you until you learn English,'" Desi recalled.

Although he'd studied English in Cuba, Desi had never spoken or read it outside the classroom. "To please Dad, I tried to answer him in English, but nothing too good came out. My ears eventually got used to it pretty well, but my tongue has been fighting a losing battle ever since," he said decades later.

The ex-mayor of Santiago [Desi's father] was staying at a boardinghouse on the outskirts of Miami while he and two other refugees started up an import business that supplied ceramic tiling to the building trade. Unable to get credit and with sparse capital of their own, they could only purchase a few hundred dollars' worth of stock at a time, which meant it all had to be sold before they could buy any more.

Desi's mother, accustomed to living like a queen, elected to stay with relatives in Santiago until her husband could support the three of them. She sent Desi on ahead to continue his education. While it now seemed impossible for him to attend Notre Dame, he could at least finish high school in America and get on with his new life.

Struggling with English

Desi plainly needed all the guidance he could get. In 1934, Miami only had a small Hispanic population; on his first solo visit to a restaurant, Desi couldn't read the menu or understand the waitress. In embarrassment, he just pointed to four items and ended up with four different bowls of soup. He consumed them as nonchalantly as possible to give the impression that he dined that way all the time.

Through the benevolence of [exiled dictator Gerardo] Machado, who reportedly left Cuba with $10 million in gold bullion, Desi's father arranged for him to spend the summer learning English at St. Leo's Catholic School near Tampa. Still unable to understand most of what was said to him, Desi usually answered "Yeah" or "O.K." to every-thing. One day he unintentionally volunteered for a box-ing match and received such a beating that he couldn't eat solid food for two weeks.

In the autumn of 1934, Desi entered St. Patrick's High School in Miami Beach. As an economy measure, he and his father moved out of their five-dollar-a-week boarding-house and into the warehouse of Arnaz's import company. They shifted the ceramic tiles to one half of the forty-by-forty-foot area and equipped the other half with two beds, several chairs, a wardrobe, and a two-burner stove. For plumbing, they had to rely on the toilet and sink in the of-fice next door. Rats were a constant menace. They kept baseball bats beside their beds to ward them off.

After school hours, Desi worked for his father's com-pany. At one point, Pan American Importing and Export-ing tried to diversify with bananas. The fruit could be pur-chased in Puerto Rico at three for a nickel and resold in Miami at five cents each. It seemed like a quick way to get rich, but then Desi went to the docks to pick up the latest shipment. The bananas had been too long at sea and had turned rotten.

Earning a Living

Arnaz's two partners left the bankrupted company, but he tried to carry on alone selling tiles that he imported from Mexico. Stuck with too many broken and unmatched pieces, he had the smart idea of cementing them together to create artistic effects around doorways and fireplaces. Builders of Miami apartment houses were quick to scoop them up when told it was the latest decorating craze in Latin America.

Arnaz discovered that he could get more money for the fragments than he could for whole tiles. It became his son's job to "manufacture" them. As soon as they received a new order, Desi would load the required number of tiles on the back of the delivery truck and drive through bumpy back streets until all were broken.

Desi and his father now earned enough to eat better, but they still couldn't afford to move from the warehouse or send for Mrs. Arnaz. To build up savings, Desi took a part-time job for a man who raised canaries and sold them on consignment in drugstores scattered around the Miami area. Depending on the bird's pedigree, shoppers could buy a package deal including cage, instruction book, and a month's supply of feed for $4.99 up to $24.99. For a salary of fifteen dollars a week, Desi traveled from store to store every day to feed the canaries, clean the cages, and replace depleted stock.

Making Friends

At St. Patrick's High School, Desi fell in with a crowd of rich kids who seemed to accept him as an equal. His best friend was Alphonse Capone Jr., son of the underworld kingpin, whose father was then serving an eleven-year sentence in Alcatraz for income tax evasion. Young Capone and his mother lived in great luxury in an island enclave off Miami Beach, and frequently invited Desi to be their guest. Little did anyone know that Desi was also soaking up atmosphere for a future television series he would produce, *The Untouchables*.

Desi no longer had the carte blanche of a mayor's son in bordellos, but with his sleek handsomeness and big brown eyes he had no difficulty attracting women. The nearest thing he had to a steady sweetheart was Gabriella Barreras, granddaughter of a Machado official who had the foresight to transfer his considerable fortune to an American bank *before* fleeing Cuba.

Alberto Barreras sympathized with the Arnazes' financial plight and frequently invited father and son to dinner at his mansion in Biscayne Bay. Taking a shine to Desi, Barreras remembered him when a musician friend asked if he knew any young Cubans who might be interested in a job with the resident band at the Roney Plaza Hotel.

Up to then, Desi had never considered a career in show business. Like most Cuban boys, he learned to perform serenades on the guitar at an early age, but mainly as an adjunct to romancing the opposite sex. His guitar had been destroyed in the pillage of the family's hacienda, but he'd managed to buy one secondhand for five dollars in a Miami pawnshop.

Show Business Beckons

Since Desi earned only fifteen dollars a week cleaning birdcages, he leaped at the chance to bring home thirty-nine dollars a week for entertaining, which he happily would have done for free. He passed the Roney Plaza audition easily, but had trouble gaining his father's consent. Desiderio II still had hopes of Desi becoming a lawyer; performing in dimly lighted nightspots seemed just a notch above gangsterism or pimping. But he couldn't quibble with the thirty-nine dollars a week, which would improve their standard of living considerably.

Though Desi was still in his senior year in high school, the working schedule presented no conflict. The Siboney Septet played seven nights a week at the Roney Plaza, plus a Sunday afternoon tea dance. Since the Roney Plaza ranked as the top hotel in Miami Beach at the time, it was a lucky break for Desi. The Siboney Septet, which consisted of a singer-guitarist (counted as two people!), pianist, maraca shaker, bassist, and two bongo players, was a relief group that performed between sets of the stellar name band on the bill. During that winter of 1936, the headline attraction was the orchestra of Charles "Buddy" Rogers, the wavy-haired actor-singer-bandleader who had just become engaged to silent-movie queen Mary Pickford.

The Siboney Septet specialized in the rumba, one of the most graceful of all ballroom dances. Women loved the rumba because it showed off their whirling skirts and ankles to good effect, but men shied away because it seemed too hard to master. The dance floor would be packed when Buddy Rogers's band played their repertoire of swing tunes and foxtrots, but diners usually returned to their tables while the Siboney Septet performed.

Fearing that he'd soon lose his new job if the crowd didn't get up and dance, Desi persuaded Buddy Rogers to end his sets with "The Peanut Vendor," a novelty hit that could be played in a variety of tempos. As the Siboney Septet replaced Rogers's musicians on the bandstand, they began playing the same song, but as a rumba.

"It worked, because all of a sudden people realized they were dancing to a rumba and then decided it was not so difficult after all. They kept dancing, and that was what we were being paid to make them do," Desi recalled.

Immigration Troubles

But in the midst of success, a sudden visit from a United States Immigration officer nearly ended in the deportation of Desi and his father. Although the Arnazes had been in Miami for over two years, they had not filed for residency papers and were not permitted to work without them. Reviewing the case and realizing how much the family had lost in the 1933 revolution, the agency gave them the option of getting the required permits within ninety days or being sent back to Cuba.

It was easier said than done. The Arnazes could only obtain permanent residency by filing at an American consulate *outside* the United States. Fearful that he might land back in prison if he returned to Cuba, Desiderio II took a cheap steamer to Puerto Rico and applied there.

When his father's mission was successfully completed two weeks later, Desi boarded the ferry to Havana to get his own papers. While back in the homeland, he persuaded his mother to file for U.S. residency as well. She followed him to Miami several weeks later.

A gang of Desi's schoolmates decided to surprise him when he ended his enforced leave of absence and rejoined the Siboney Septet during one of the Roney Plaza's Sunday afternoon tea dances. Nearly packing the room, the teenagers pretended to be bored by Buddy Rogers's orchestra but became wildly attentive when Desi's group started playing. They all jumped up from their tables and danced, pausing to cheer and applaud whenever Desi sang.

Cugat Takes Notice

The ovation had the desired effect on Desi's ego, but it also attracted the attention of Xavier Cugat, who was on a busman's holiday during an afternoon off from an engagement at the ultrachic Brook Club. Until a waiter pointed Cugat out, Desi didn't recognize the balding, mustachioed man, who was that era's "king" of Latin dance music.

Desi's swollen ego told him that Cugat wanted to congratulate him on his performance. He strolled by the maestro's table several times, even stopped right in front of him and lighted a cigarette to attract his attention, but he got no reaction. Just as he was packing up his guitar to leave, he heard Cugat call, "Hey, Chico! Come over here, please."

The following afternoon, Desi found himself auditioning for Cugat at the Brook Club. The bandleader asked him if he knew "In Spain They Say Si Si." Desi did, although he'd never actually performed it with the Siboney Septet. Cugat told Desi to attempt it anyway.

Desi was petrified, but when the band set down a torrid beat the likes of which he hadn't heard since leaving

Santiago, he felt like he was home again. "My Cuban blood was flowing," Desi recollected. "My hips were revolving, my feet were kicking, my arms were waving. By comparison, Elvis Presley would have looked as if he were standing still. I sang the [heck] out of that song."

When Desi finished, the musicians applauded. Not one to waste words, Cugat offered him a job, only to be rejected. Desi knew that his parents would never let him accept until he graduated from high school in June. Even then it would be a tough battle convincing them.

"Well, if you're still interested, write to me at the Waldorf-Astoria in New York," Cugat said.

When graduation finally came around, Desi did contact Cugat, but without informing his parents. He figured that the bandleader would have forgotten him by that time, but he got a surprise. Cugat offered him a two-week trial at twenty-five dollars per week, plus one-way bus fare to New York. . . .

Desi Makes His Debut

Desi made his Cugat debut under rather intimidating circumstances—in a 10,000-seat outdoor amphitheater in Cleveland, Ohio, in, [showman] Billy Rose's *Aquacade*, which was water show, vaudeville, and musical combined into one colossal spectacle with a cast of 500. Olympic champions Eleanor Holm and Buster Crabbe were the swimming stars, flanked by a hundred AquaBelles and Beaux.

Cugat's orchestra performed on an elevated stage at one end of an artificial lake. While singing "In Spain They Say Si Si" for the first time, Desi nearly skidded off the platform into the water, but one of the dancers grabbed him by the scruff of the neck in time.

Desi passed the two-week trial period and found his salary raised to thirty dollars a week, still less than he'd been earning with the Siboney Septet. After *Aquacade*, the Cugat contingent moved on to the Arrowhead Inn in Saratoga, New York, then in the height of its annual thoroughbred racing season, which attracted sportsmen and celebrities from all over the country.

Bing Crosby, America's number-one crooner and horse fancier, came to see the show one night and enjoyed Desi's singing so much that he invited him for a drink afterwards. Crosby happened to ask Desi how much Cugat paid him. When told, he said, "Why that cheap crook!"

Crosby sent for Cugat and read him the riot act. The bandleader replied, "But he's just starting out, Bingo."

"Never mind the Bingo stuff, you stingy Spaniard," Crosby said. "Give him a raise. One of these days you're going to be asking *him* for a job!"

Cugat finally conceded when Crosby agreed to sing with the orchestra. Crosby loved Latin music, so he obliged with several numbers and dueted with Desi on "Quiereme Mucho."

"Bing sang it in Spanish, which he knew pretty good, and then I did it in my version of English, which was pretty bad. But the Bacardi rum we'd been drinking helped a lot," Desi remembered.

Xavier Cugat kept his part of the bargain by raising Desi's salary to thirty-five dollars a week. For the extra five dollars, Desi also had to walk Cugat's dogs—two Mexican Chihuahuas and a German shepherd—three times a day. . . .

Moving Up

Desi was quick to emulate Xavier Cugat's sartorial elegance and impeccable grooming. On stage, Cugat was famed for wearing huge sombreros, with a vividly colored serape draped over his tuxedo and a Chihuahua cradled in his arms. Unlike Cugat, twenty-year-old Desi had no problem with premature baldness, but a few strands of his black hair had turned gray, perhaps due to the trauma of the family's flight from Cuba. Cugat recommended that he start tinting it, which Desi did until well into middle age, when he gradually stopped and let his hair go natural again.

From Cugat, Desi also learned the importance of putting on a show rather than a performance. The Cugat orchestra became popular not only for its music but for production numbers with gorgeously costumed singers, dancers, and musicians. Realizing that many in the audience might not know the samba or the rumba or the tango, Cugat always had choristers doing the steps on stage so that people on the dance floor could learn by watching them.

After six months, Desi realized that he'd advanced about as far as he could with Xavier Cugat. The undisputed drawing card of the unit, Cugat had been getting a bit touchy about the ovations that Desi received in his next-to-closing spot. Also, Cugat refused to raise Desi's salary even one cent above thirty-five dollars a week. In those days, Cugat could get away with low wages because lesser instrumentalists, singers, and dancers weren't protected by the musicians' union. That was the main reason why he could maintain such a large group.

When the orchestra returned to pricey New York for a month's engagement at the Waldorf-Astoria, Desi discovered that he could barely survive on thirty-five dollars a week. "Having to go through the Waldorf kitchen to get to the bandstand helped," he recalled. "I lifted all the food I could and stashed it into my rumba shirt every time we passed through for our ten-minute break. Those wide, full sleeves with all the big ruffles were very useful."

While leaving work at 2:30 A.M. one night, Desi asked Cugat if they could stop at the coffee shop for breakfast and a chat. As soon as they'd ordered, Desi announced that he intended to return to Miami to form a small group similar to the Siboney Septet. "I know just as much as that guy who was the leader—a lot more, really, thanks to you—but

I just can't make enough money with you," he told Cugat.

Cugat sensed another maneuver for a pay raise and didn't bite. "You won't have a chance," he said. "There's not many people who know and like Latin music in this country yet. You'll have a tough time. You'll go hungry."

"Well, dammit, Cugie, I'm hungry now," Desi replied. "Besides, my mother and father are there. Maybe I'll fall on my ass, but I've got to try it."

The skinflint bandleader astounded Desi with a sudden burst of generosity. "Okay, I'll do what I can to help you get started. You can bill yourself as Desi Arnaz and his Xavier Cugat Orchestra direct from the Waldorf-Astoria Hotel in New York City. How's that?"

"That's great! Marvelous! Thank you!" Desi said. To show his appreciation, he offered to pay Cugat a royalty for the use of his name, which is probably what the maestro had in mind anyway.

Cugat leaned forward and anxiously rubbed his hands. "How much?"

"The same as you paid me when I started, twenty-five dollars a week. And like you told me then, if we do good, we'll renegotiate," Desi replied.

Cugat knew when he'd been aced. Laughing, he said, "All right . . . let's see what you can do."

Jorge Mas Canosa: Crusader for a Free Cuba

Ann Louise Bardach

Even as a teenager in Cuba, Jorge Mas Canosa was a political activist. When he was exiled to the United States, his political passion focused on overthrowing Fidel Castro. In the following selection, Ann Louise Bardach tells how Mas Canosa formed the Cuban American National Foundation (CANF), an organization whose purpose was to support the U.S. government's policies toward Cuba, with the ultimate goal of ousting Castro. The author shows that Mas Canosa was always controversial and sometimes had suspicious motives. However, she concludes, his impact on exile politics was profound. Bardach is an award-winning journalist and an expert on Cuba. She is also the author of *Cuba: A Traveler's Literary Companion*.

"We will never forget our friends," Jorge Mas Canosa was wont to say, "and we will always remember our enemies." And no one ever doubted the steadfastness of his memory. On August 19, 1994, Jorge Mas Canosa sauntered out of the White House Cabinet Room following a ninety-minute meeting with the President of the United States. He was irrepressibly gleeful. The controversial tycoon, who had long dominated South Florida politics from the bully pulpit of his Cuban American National Foundation, had just

Ann Louise Bardach, *Cuba Confidential: Love and Vengeance in Miami and Havana*. New York: Random House, 2002. Copyright © 2002 by Ann Louise Bardach. Reproduced by permission of Random House, Inc., and in the United Kingdom by the author.

pulled off another coup. A little more than three years later, Mas Canosa would be felled by cancer, but in his last years, with the acquiescence of Bill Clinton, he would reformulate America's Cuba policy, recalibrating its tone to that of the height of the Cold War. . . .

Like the majority of Cubans, Jorge Mas Canosa was industrious and hardworking, starting out as a dishwasher at the Fontainebleau hotel in Miami and later working as a milkman. At the time of his death at the age of fifty-eight, Mas Canosa was worth well in excess of $400 million. His company, MasTec Inc., formed in 1994 by acquiring a competitor, was valued at over $700 million. When he wasn't globetrotting drumming up anti-Castro support or lobbying for business contracts, he lived with his wife, Irma, behind electric gates in a large but shapeless home in Pinecrest, a suburb in southwestern Miami. Perched on the roof was a huge satellite dish, and he told friends that inside he had a state-of-the-art communications system and was ready to take over the command of Cuba at a moment's notice.

An Early Passion for Politics

Jorge Mas Canosa was born in Santiago de Cuba in 1939, one of five children. The son of a career army officer and veterinarian, he early on developed a passion for intrigue and politics. His younger brother, Ricardo, recalled a terrifying day in 1956 in Santiago when Rolando Masferrer and his Tigres, the dreaded paramilitary group active during the [Fulgencio] Batista years, stormed and ransacked their family home. "Jorge was doing counterrevolutionary work," recounted Ricardo, who said they were probably spared a worse fate due to their father's status in the army. "My father was in the military and they told him that he had seventy-two hours to get Jorge out of the country."

Mas Canosa's father, Ramón Emilio Mas, hustled him

out of Cuba and enrolled him at Presbyterian Junior College in Maxton, North Carolina, in 1956. By all accounts, Mas Canosa's father was well regarded and not averse to taking personal risks. Two unrelated men told me in Havana in the mid-1990s that Mas Canosa's father had engineered their release from the Moncada garrison, where they were certain to face torture and probable death. Mas Canosa returned to Santiago a week after Castro seized power in early January 1959, and briefly attended law school at Oriente University. But he soon fell afoul of the new government and was arrested for plastering anti-Castro stickers on buildings. Mas Canosa often regaled friends with the story of his arrest. "God came to my rescue. I delivered a beautiful piece of oratory," he said. His fervor and loquaciousness so impressed his captors that they released him.

On July 15, 1960, Mas Canosa fled to Miami and immediately hooked up with several of the dozens of CIA-financed anti-Castro groups in South Florida. He would play a supporting role in the Bay of Pigs invasion as squad leader of a diversionary unit called El Grupo Niño Díaz, which returned to Miami once the invasion was deemed a failure. Following the Bay of Pigs debacle, Mas Canosa enlisted in the U.S. Army; he was accepted as an officer candidate and was eventually commissioned as a second lieutenant. While the majority of Cuban recruits were dispatched to Fort Knox or Fort Jackson, he was dispatched to Fort Benning, which trained the exile elite, instructing them in intelligence, clandestine operations and propaganda. At Fort Benning, he became close to two men who would remain lifelong friends and associates: Félix Rodríguez and Luis Posada Carriles, both CIA assets intermittently through the [1983–1986] Iran-Contra affair. The former would participate in the murder of [revolutionary] Che Guevara; the latter would be Fidel Castro's most persistent would-be assassin. When it became clear that a second invasion of Cuba would never happen, Mas Canosa returned to Miami.

In 1961, he married Irma Santos, his high school sweetheart from Santiago. The couple had three sons, all of whom would eventually work at their father's company. In the early 1960s Mas Canosa became deeply involved in another CIA-backed group, RECE (Cuban Representation in Exile), and, according to his brother, its military arm, CORU (Commandos of the United Revolutionary Organizations), an alliance of twenty men from the most extreme anti-Castro groups run by dedicated militants such as Orlando Bosch, Luis Posada Carriles and Ignacio and Guillermo Novo. . . .

The Founding of CANF

By the late '70s, Mas Canosa realized that paramilitary strikes against Cuba were unlikely to topple Castro on their own. He became keenly interested in American politics and threw his explosive energy behind the 1980 Florida Senate campaign of Paula Hawkins, who coattailed to victory on the [President Ronald] Reagan landslide. When she won, he virtually "parked himself" in her Senate office, according to a former CANF director. Using his influence with Hawkins, Mas Canosa won introductions to some of the key players in the Reagan administration—among them Richard Allen, Reagan's first National Security Adviser. It was Allen who came up with the brainstorm of forming a Cuban-American organization that would advance and popularize the administration's agenda and policies in Latin America while at the same time burnishing Cuban-Americans' own image and legitimacy. In March 1981, Mas Canosa co-founded the Cuban American National Foundation with two prominent exile businessmen and activists, Raúl Masvidal and Carlos Salman, both of whom were better known than he at the time.

CANF was modeled on the powerful Israeli lobby with

the help of Washington attorney Barney Barnett, who had formed AIPAC (the American Israel Public Affairs Committee). Barnett introduced the men to Tom Dine, AIPAC's executive director, and counseled them on the mechanics of forming a nonprofit, a PAC [political action committee] and a lobbying entity. Fourteen Miami businessmen were the founding members. Their charter was based on a proposal drafted by Frank Calzón, who would serve as the new foundation's first executive director.

CANF moved into a Miami building that was built by Church & Tower, according to Ricardo Mas Canosa, who said he supervised its construction. Later, CANF leased tony glass offices in Washington overlooking the Potomac, eventually purchasing a landmark building off Embassy Row. Until 2000, CANF enjoyed nonprofit, tax-exempt status while securing vast sums of fungible government grants. Its various umbrellas and PACs, like the Free Cuba Committee, paid out much of its assets to favored politicians and causes. From 1981 until his death, reported Gaeton Fonzi, a Mas Canosa chronicler, more than $200 million of taxpayer money ended up financing Mas Canosa's crusade to topple Fidel Castro.

Known as "the Foundation" in Miami and Washington, CANF received between $5,000 and $50,000 in annual dues from those sitting on its board of directors and from its trustees. Virtually every Florida politician since CANF's inception has been enriched by hefty contributions, notably Ileana Ros-Lehtinen, Lincoln Díaz-Balart, former Senator Connie Mack, the late Governor Lawton Chiles, and former Congressmen Dante Fascell and the late Claude Pepper, as well as out-of-staters such as New Jersey's Robert Torricelli and Robert Menéndez and Senator Fritz Hollings of North Carolina—all of whom proved to be reliable pit bulls for CANF. "The Israeli lobby buys Democrats and rents Republicans," quipped one former

Bush official. "The Cubans buy Republicans and rent Democrats.". . .

Debating Mas Canosa's Role

Since Mas Canosa's death [from lung cancer in 1997], there has been contentious debate over his role and loss to the exile world. Certainly, no one has filled his shoes. His old friend Luis Posada Carriles lamented his passing and fretted that the anti-Castro movement was rudderless and drifting. "Right now is a bad time," said Posada, a year after his friend's death. "Too many years. Everybody is very old." Posada said he had last spoken with Mas Canosa about a month before his death. "He was very sick then," he said. "It was very sad. He was in terrible pain. He knew he was dying. He was a very powerful man." Posada paused and shook his head ruefully. "Now is nothing."

In his abbreviated life, from the founding of CANF in 1981, Mas Canosa set the tone and the agenda for America's foreign policy with Cuba: no compromise, no negotiation—a policy of slow strangulation. But toward the end, he showed a willingness to confront his enemy. In September 1996, a year before he died, Mas Canosa took a dangerous gamble and went on live Spanish language television to debate Ricardo Alarcón, the president of Cuba's National Assembly. For years, Mas had railed against *dialogueros*. Now he would be dialoguing with the man who was number two in the Cuban government. Although there was no definitive winner, he was uncharacteristically restrained. He comported himself well and made his points succinctly, surprising both his critics and supporters.

An adroit strategist, Mas Canosa was a pragmatist who eschewed battles he could not win.

Celia Cruz: Queen of Salsa

Lydia Martin

Growing up poor in Cuba, Celia Cruz entered singing con-
tests as a young girl to win prizes that often consisted of
food—a commodity that was much needed by her family.
In the following selection, author Lydia Martin tells how
Cruz rose to stardom in her native Cuba, but left the country to escape the repressive regime of Fidel Castro. Like
most other Cuban exiles, she believed her flight was temporary, yet she never again returned to the Cuba she loved.
Instead, she remained in the United States and achieved
worldwide fame by creating a modern sound called salsa.
As the author notes, by the time of Cruz's death in 2003,
she had taken her Cuban salsa to every corner of the globe.
Martin is a writer who contributes stories about cultural
icons to *Hispanic* magazine.

Three years ago [in 2000], Celia Cruz, the undisputed
Queen of Salsa, an icon to generation after generation,
broke down in a Miami recording studio.

In a voice that after six decades of stardom and more
than 76 recordings had lost some of its highest ranges but
none of its soulful power, she did take after take of "Por
Si Acaso No Regreso" (In Case I Don't Return), an ode to
Cuba written for her by music mogul and fellow Cuban
American Emilio Estefan.

"It was hard to finish recording that song. We had to

keep stopping, because she would start crying," said Estefan, one of the organizers of Cruz's Miami memorial on July 19 [2003], three days after her death to brain cancer. She was 77.

Thousands of Hispanics from every part of the world waved their native flags and shouted chants of "Celia" as her body made its way from the Freedom Tower in Miami and New York's Saint Patrick's Cathedral the next day in two very visible memorials. Critics are comparing the events to the day Elvis Presley died.

Cruz Yearned for Cuba

Even as she made a new life for herself in the United States, Cruz never stopped yearning for her homeland.

"I never wanted to abandon you. I took you with me with each step," sings the song she finally managed to record for Estefan in a voice that sounds uncharacteristically pained. It's on *Siempre Viviré* (I Will Always Live), a CD released in 2000. "If I don't return to my land, remember that I loved her with my life," she sings.

When Cruz left Cuba in 1960 to escape the communist regime that shackled free expression, she was one of her country's biggest and dearest stars. Like most Cubans who left in those days, she expected her exile would be temporary. But four decades later, Fidel Castro is still in power and Cruz died without ever again glimpsing her hometown. (Once, in 1990, she returned to the U.S. Guantanamo Base on the island for a concert.)

Cruz was already well known throughout the Latin world, but after landing in New York's Latin jazz scene and hooking up with the late Tito Puente, the Puerto Rican percussionist and bandleader who was helping create a modern sound called salsa, her star began climbing higher.

By the end of her life, she had taken Cuban music, the root of salsa, to every corner of the globe. She had won two Grammys and three Latin Grammys. She had worked with some of the music world's biggest names, from Luciano Pavarotti and Gloria Estefan to Patti Labelle and Wyclef Jean. She had recorded with all the salsa greats and appeared in several movies, including *The Mambo Kings* and *The Perez Family.*

She had accepted honorary degrees from Yale, the University of Miami and Florida International University. She had scored a star on Hollywood's Walk of Fame and Miami's Calle Ocho, been immortalized in wax and presented by President Bill Clinton with the National Endowment for the Arts award.

But still Cruz refused to slow down. Until December [2002], when she underwent surgery to remove a brain tumor, she was touring the world more than 11 months out of the year. Her concerts sold out in Latin America, Japan, Thailand, Morocco, Ireland, Denmark, England, Germany.

Fame Never Went to Her Head

Despite the long hours, Cruz, well into her 70s, had the stamina that fails young rock stars. She never threatened to spiral out of control from the demands of fame. She never needed to crawl under a rock somewhere for a couple of years to escape the punishments of a public life. And that's because she had a simple, genuine passion for her art—rare in the modern world of multimillion-dollar record deals.

"You never saw a picture of that woman where she wasn't smiling," said Greta Roblanes, 43, who waited four hours in the sweltering Miami heat to pay her respects. "You got the sense that she was filled with joy every time she went on stage. And she transmitted that to her audience."

Whenever media asked Cruz why she refused to retire, she would say, "I can't retire because without the stage I'd die."

But the truth was more practical. Unlike other artists who retired to their mansions, Cruz—even after knee surgery in 2000 forced her to abandon her trademark six-inch heels, so famous the Smithsonian has a pair—performed on stage.

"Well, for one thing, they're millionaires" Cruz said. "I keep going on stage because I'm not. My audiences are poor. They can't pay $50 or $60 to see me perform. I work because . . . I have to."

But the testament to her artistic integrity is her last recording, *Regalo del Alma* (Gift from the Soul), released after her death and which Cruz finished after being sent home from the hospital. The first print of the CD was buried with her in the Bronx, along with a jar of Cuban soil.

"She really insisted on finishing that record," said her manager Omar Pardillo, whom Cruz loved as a son. She and her husband of 41 years, Pedro Knight, never had children.

Simplicity Was a Way of Life

The two met in the sizzling Havana of the 1950s, when he played trumpet and she sang for La Sonora Matancera, one of Cuba's hottest bands. They were inseparable until the end.

Cruz and her "cabecita de algodón [little cotton head]," as she called him, traveled the globe together and retained a relationship free of scandal. Knight was famous for never failing to open car doors for his wife and always holding her hand when they crossed the street. Cruz never failed to remind him to take his insulin shots three times a day, even in the middle of interviews.

They were rarely home in Fort Lee, N.J., but when they were, she pressed his clothes and cooked him diabetic-friendly meals. He made her morning coffee. "If he doesn't make the coffee, I won't drink it," she said.

Perhaps Cruz retained her simplicity because she never hankered for stardom. She grew up poor in the Havana neighborhood of Santos Suárez. A tourist bought her first pair of shoes after she belted out an impressive song. As a teen, she sang her younger siblings to sleep with the front door open to allow for the tropical breeze. But when neighbors started crowding around to listen, she'd shut the door.

In the late 1940s, a cousin talked her into competing in an amateur radio contest and she won. "I really loved to sing," she told reporters. "But I also did it because if you won, you would get a cake, or a bag with chocolate, condensed milk, ham. We were very poor. All of that came in very handy at home."

All the while, she was studying to be a schoolteacher. But upon graduation, a teacher told her, "You just keep singing."

So she kept singing. La Sonora Matancera, perhaps the island's most popular band at the time, came calling in 1950. In 1960, she left Cuba with the band to perform in Mexico—and never returned.

In the 1960s, she set New York's Palladium on fire with Tito Puente. But in 1962, she got a devastating telegram. Her mother had died in Cuba. Cruz yearned to return for her mother's funeral. But the Cuban government, which never forgave her for defecting, refused to let her in.

"Not being able to attend her mother's funeral was the greatest pain in her life and she carried it until the end," said trumpet great Alfredo "Chocolate" Armenteros. "I was there the day the Cuban government turned her down. She was inconsolable."

If something piqued Celia, it was that the Cuban government tried to erase her from the collective memory. Her records ware considered contraband and her name didn't appear in music books after the revolution. But she remained a household name on the island anyway, a boot-legged star whose homemade tapes blasted from stereos all over the island upon her death.

"Celia is the kind of star that cannot be equaled," said Dominican bandleader Johnny Pacheco. "She was unique in every way. There will never be another Celia Cruz."

Orlando "El Duque" Hernández: Star of the Yankees

Steve Fainaru and Ray Sánchez

Orlando "El Duque" Hernández was a star baseball player in Cuba. But in 1996 Fidel Castro banned El Duque from baseball for allegedly planning to defect to the United States. Unable to play the game he loved, he hatched a risky plan. In December 1997, two friends with a boat delivered him and several others to Anguilla Cay, and friends still in Cuba agreed to alert the U.S. Coast Guard to the refugees' whereabouts. The boat owners then returned to Cuba unnoticed. The execution of the plan was not flawless; Hernández and the others were stranded for three days before being spotted by a Coast Guard helicopter and rescued. During a short stay in Costa Rica, Hernández signed a contract with the New York Yankees in February 1998, came to the United States, and achieved almost instantaneous fame and fortune. In the following selection, sportswriters Steve Fainaru and Ray Sánchez recount the story of Hernández: the journey of a refugee from desperate circumstances to a new life as a top pitcher for the Yankees. Steve Fainaru is an investigative sportswriter for the *Washington Post*, and Ray Sánchez writes a column for *Newsday*.

The Yankee first-base coach happened to be Cuban: a former major-league outfielder named José Cardenal. In the operation of a great and powerful baseball machine, Car-

Steve Fainaru and Ray Sánchez, *The Duke of Havana: Baseball, Cuba, and the Search for the American Dream*. New York: Villard Books, 2001. Copyright © 2001 by Steve Fainaru and Ray Sánchez. Reproduced by permission of Alfred A. Knopf, Inc., a division of Random House, Inc.

denal played a relatively minor role. Many fans had no idea
who the Yankee first-base coach even was. But Cardenal became appreciably more important with El Duque's [Or-
lando Hernández's] arrival [in 1997]. Among other things,
he was the only Yankee who remotely understood the
complexity of the pitcher's transition from pariah of the
Cuban revolution to emerging star on the most famous
team in American sports.

Cardenal had grown up in Matanzas, the province directly east of Havana. His father was a black carpenter who
earned $5 a week. His mother was a white housekeeper. The
family resided in a one-room apartment with a concrete floor
and two beds: one for Cardenal, his father and two brothers,
the other for his mother and two sisters. The apartment was
part of a sweltering complex of brick and rock equipped
with one communal outhouse for six families.

Cardenal's memory was still scarred by the embedded
racism of prerevolutionary Cuba. More than four decades
later, he could instantly recall the names of the pristine
beaches and glittery private clubs he had been forbidden
to enter. As a boy, one of his favorite pastimes was to hurl
rocks through the windows of the Casino Español, a
whites-only club whose uniformed attendants often kicked
him off the sidewalk. "We'd break the windows and take
off running," he said. "I was one of the leaders. There
were six or seven of us. We hated the way they treated us,
we just hated them."

Baseball Was a Way Out of Poverty

From an early age Cardenal saw baseball as a way to tran-
scend the poverty and racism that surrounded him. In
1954 his brother Pedro signed with the St. Louis Cardinals
and started sending back $50 each month to help his fam-
ily. On weekends Cardenal's father would take him by train
into Havana to watch the Cuban professional league. After

the games Cardenal would stand in the parking lot and watch the players drive away in their Cadillac convertibles. Among them was the national hero, Orestes "Minnie" Miñoso, who played for the Chicago White Sox during the summer. Cardenal couldn't help but notice that Miñoso was even blacker than he was. "He always drove a white Cadillac," Cardenal recalled. "And he always had three blondes in the backseat."

"I'm going to park my convertible right over there," Cardenal told his father.

Then, in the first hours of 1959, the triumphant caravan that carried Fidel Castro to power snaked through Matanzas on its way to Havana. Cardenal and his family stood in the blockaded streets, cheering as the charismatic thirty-two-year-old leader passed by. Fidel had fought for people like the Cardenals: the poor and the black and the marginalized. Their lives could only get better. Two years later, Cardenal signed with the San Francisco Giants for $250, joining his cousin Bert Campaneris, Tony Pérez, Tony Oliva and Luis Tiant as part of the last wave of Cuban ballplayers to migrate legally to the United States. Cardenal thought that, like his hero Miñoso, he would return home every winter. From his meager signing bonus, he gave $50 to his father and $50 to his mother. He used $100 to buy a new suit and a new glove. The other $50 he took with him to the States, where he played eighteen seasons in the major leagues. He didn't return to Cuba until his father's death in 1984.

Cardenal often said that he would never have taken the same risks as El Duque to play major-league baseball. "You have to ask yourself what's more important: freedom or death," he said. "For him it was freedom. For me it would be death." Cardenal was immensely proud of El Duque, as a Cuban and as a ballplayer. He was in awe of the pitcher's inner strength, his confidence and serenity on the mound.

Most of all he could empathize with El Duque's poor up-bringing. . . . Cardenal sought to help ease El Duque into his new life and shield him from the distractions that came with being a professional athlete.

Transition Was Hard

For the growing legions of Latin Americans in the major leagues, the transition to professional baseball was dramatic. Many players did not speak English. The economic pressures—to lift one's family out of life-threatening poverty—were enormous. The temptations were constant. As [sportswriter] Marcos Bretón has written, cities like New York are littered with ex-ballplayers, their visas expired, their dreams and signing bonuses long gone. But El Duque carried with him a more unique burden of the Latin American experience: the legacy of communism. He had come from a place where friends, neighbors and even teammates informed on one another. "The big secret about repression in Cuba is that it's internal, it's psychological," said Jorge Morejón, a former journalist for Prensa Latina, the Cuban news agency. By the time El Duque arrived in the States, he had seen the capriciousness of success. In a New York minute his life had been torn apart over issues well beyond his control, issues of global politics and ideology. Inside Cuba it was widely assumed—although never proven—that his best friend, Germán Mesa, had helped precipitate his downfall.[1] By nature, El Duque was private and suspicious, with a Cuban predilection to *discutir*, to argue, everything under the sun. He brought this baggage into the New York Yankee clubhouse and the world's largest media market.

"It was very hard for him in the beginning; the changes in his life were so drastic," said infielder Luis Sojo, who be-

1. Mesa was suspected of spreading the story that Hernández planned to defect, which caused El Duque to be banned from baseball in Cuba.

came one of his closest friends on the team. Within a year El Duque's combativeness would subside to the point where it was only occasionally an issue. In those first weeks, however, he seemed to fight constant battles. In a way, it was something of a paradox. El Duque's teammates, to a man, accorded him immense respect. The media, after months covering a powerful yet colorless team, feasted on his amazing story. The fans immediately adored him. Yet he seemed to see enemies lurking around every corner. . . .

Tempers Flare

Some of El Duque's most furious battles were with his new catcher, Jorge Posada. Normally, rookie pitchers are more than content to let the catcher or the bench call the pitches. El Duque shook off Posada in his very first game. The tension was immediate. Posada was the son of a Cuban father, a ballplayer who had fled the revolution, and a Puerto Rican mother. He was born and raised in Puerto Rico. Generally speaking, the relationship between the two islands is a complicated one, fused with strong feelings about independence and sovereignty. José Martí, Cuba's poet and independence hero, famously called Cuba and Puerto Rico "two wings of the same bird." And yet after the Spanish-American War, Cuba gained its independence from Spain while Puerto Rico was handed over to the United States, of which it remains a commonwealth.

All of which is probably beside the point, but El Duque and Posada battled each other like brothers. Similar in temperament, stubborn, both had something to prove. Posada would later become an all-star, but at this point he was still trying to establish himself as the Yankees' everyday catcher. And here was El Duque, a rookie—a thirty-two-year-old rookie, but still a rookie—challenging his pitch selection. In context, it was no small matter. The fundamental issue was who controlled the game: the pitcher or the catcher.

Posada stormed out to the mound one afternoon during a game against the Marlins. "I kept calling for a pitch and he kept shaking me off," said Posada. "I don't remember what the pitch was, but I walked out there and I said, 'Look, you have to throw this!' And he said, 'No, I'm not throwing it!' Right after that they hit a shot off of him, and when we got back to the dugout we started cursing at each other. We used every curse you can possibly imagine.". . .

"It was a growing experience for both of us," said Posada. "We both came out of it closer friends. Over time it became easier for us to talk and disagree without blowing up.". . .

El Duque Shines

El Duque spent his rookie season [of 1998] in a two-room suite at the Hotel Roger Smith at Forty-seventh Street and Lexington Avenue in Manhattan. Cardenal, who also lived there, had gotten him the room, bringing the pitcher out of his isolation at the Fort Lee Hilton. The Roger Smith, supposedly named after a mythical traveler, was small and unpretentious; it was located five blocks north of Grand Central Terminal, enabling Cardenal and El Duque to catch the number 4 subway and be at Yankee Stadium in twenty minutes.

El Duque traveled unnoticed at first, but before long his fellow commuters began to besiege him for autographs. The principal reason was that he continued to win. After his first two starts there had been some lingering skepticism, if only because the teams he had beaten, Tampa Bay and Montreal, were among the weakest in baseball. In his third start El Duque traveled to Cleveland to face the defending American League champions. There was no doubt that this would be a test. The Indians' pitching staff was young and erratic, but the batting order was loaded: Kenny Lofton, Omar Vizquel, David Justice, Manny Ramírez, Jim Thome, Travis Fryman. It went on and on. Cleveland's style was to bludgeon pitchers into submission.

It was June 18, [1998] a hot night in Cleveland, and El Duque took the mound at Jacobs Field in a turtleneck. He carried a shutout into the eighth inning. All night, he slithered in and out of desperate jams. El Duque has large hands, and at times as he threw he made the baseball seem like an egg in the hands of a magician. The third inning was typical: The Tribe put a runner on third with one out. El Duque then struck out Ramírez with a murderous slider and Thome with a change-up that had all the violent force of a Nerf ball. Thome, who would look just as comfortable hacking cordwood as he would a baseball, ripped straight through the pitch.

As the Indians' futility mounted, manager Mike Hargrove tried a novel tactic. Hargrove noticed that El Duque wiggled his fingers inside his glove when he went into the stretch. Twice he tried to argue that this behavior constituted a balk. Hargrove's tactics were pure gamesmanship, blatant attempts to unnerve an untested rookie.

As Hargrove argued, David Cone moved to the top step of the dugout.

"Hey, he came over on a boat! That's not going to scare him!" Cone yelled as the Yankee bench erupted in laughter.

The Yanks won 5-2. El Duque didn't get the win because the game was tied when he left, but no one cared. His ERA was 1.52. Now the praise was unrestrained. Cone called him "one of the most poised pitchers I've ever been around." [Manager Joe] Torre marveled: "He's just got such a calm about him." Tom Keegan, a veteran baseball writer for the [New York] Post, watched the performance with similar awe. Keegan was rarely given to oversentimentality. In 1999, when Mets manager Bobby Valentine volunteered that he should be fired if his team missed the playoffs, Keegan wrote a column beneath the headline: WHY WAIT? CAN THE PHONY NOW! But even Keegan was gushing over a pitcher with three major-league starts under his belt:

> Maybe it's the way his right knee nearly brushes his chin at the beginning of his delivery. It could be the swiftness with which he bounds off the mound and is at home plate in a flash when a runner is on third and a pitch is in the dirt. Or is it how he changes from a ground ball pitcher to a strikeout artist the moment a runner advances within 90 feet of scoring?

> So limber, so nimble, so clutch.

> Whatever the cause, Orlando "El Duque" Hernandez is a pitcher who grips an audience and forces it to watch him. He's different, from his delivery to his high socks to his myriad arm angles to his quick feet. . . .

Struggling to Adjust

In many ways El Duque remained as mysterious as on the day he arrived. He kept a respectful distance from his teammates. After games he often retreated to a Cuban diner, Mambí, which he had stumbled upon one day after getting lost on his way to Yankee Stadium while still commuting in from Jersey. The restaurant was a hole-in-the-wall at Broadway and 177th Street in Washington Heights, but it had excellent Cuban cuisine and a down-to-earth clientele. It was there that El Duque relaxed, gorging himself on comfort food: pork ribs, beans and white rice. The owner, Billy Morales, had grown up in Remedio, the same town as El Duque's father, and he and the pitcher became friends. One night after a game [coauthor Ray] Sánchez and I had dinner with El Duque at Mambí. Afterward, we all walked out onto Broadway. It was about two A.M., and in front of the restaurant on the sidewalk, two men were playing dominoes on top of a cardboard box. El Duque sat down on the curb and played for several minutes, slapping down the tiles as if he were back in Havana.

At times Sánchez and I wondered whether El Duque was entirely comfortable with his sudden wealth, his life among the privileged of capitalism. His life was certainly easier and he had more than enough toys. Instead of harassing him, the police now cut him slack as he drove like a maniac through Manhattan. He often relished the attention. But in Cuba, the distance between him and the average citizen had been not nearly as great, even during his salad days. He had had a house and certain privileges, but he had to scramble like everyone else. Roberto "Pelusa" Martínez, one of El Duque's best friends, once told me that El Duque had been "a revolutionary" in the same way that he was. They valued the revolution's achievements, the universal health care and the absence of extreme poverty and the commitment to education. They were fiercely proud of the country. "In that sense, yes, El Duque was a revolutionary," said Pelusa.

El Duque admitted that he never would have left Cuba had the government not essentially forced him out. One evening Sánchez and his girlfriend, Joyce Wong, went over to visit the pitcher at the Roger Smith. It was difficult to walk inside the small suite. The room was stuffed with the gratuitous perks of El Duque's new fame: designer sunglasses, compact-disc players, unwrapped sweaters, athletic shoes, cigars—boxes and boxes of free stuff.

"Look at all this," he said finally to Sánchez. "Look at how much I make, and I get all this . . . for nothing. You make a fraction of what I make, and you can't afford it. There's something wrong there. There's something wrong with this system."

Sánchez asked him what he meant. El Duque backed off. "Ah, you're still better off here," he said.

Dealing with the Media

Of all the changes in the pitcher's life, the constant presence of the media was perhaps the most profound. Inside
Cuba, the Communist party press had been El Duque's invisible nemesis, an instrument used by the government to
keep him down. Even when he had been a superstar he had
little contact with reporters. By design the Cuban press
tended to emphasize collective rather than individual
achievements. Thus, there were no features on the players'
private lives, no up-close-and-personal interviews, no
sportswriters asking El Duque why he had thrown a curve-
ball instead of a change-up. There were not even box
scores. After El Duque was banned he frequently raged
about the Communist media's refusal to print his version
of events. He wanted to tell the country what had happened, but no one except foreigners and friends would listen to him.

New York was at the other end of the media spectrum.
No fewer than eight newspapers and one radio station,
WFAN, traveled with the Yankees full-time. At home, the
coverage grew exponentially: fifteen papers, a dozen radio
stations, two websites and the official team magazine, not
to mention the visiting and national media. It was a small
army that gathered in the clubhouse every afternoon to
collect data on the comings and goings of the Yankee uni-
verse. The beat writers, particularly those from the
tabloids, competed fiercely over the tiniest minutiae: in-
jury updates, team meetings, trade rumors, adjustments
in the pitching rotation, September call-ups. It was the ultimate in saturation coverage.

All of this made El Duque's situation more curious. Yankee Stadium was hardly the place to keep a secret. Yet even
the most basic information about the pitcher—most notably
his age and how he arrived—remained shrouded in mystery.
El Duque was usually cordial with the writers; if he was oc-

casionally testy, there was little of the coldness that had existed with [Japanese player Hideki] Irabu (the *Post*'s George King referred to El Duque as "the anti-Irabu"). But he told them almost nothing about his pitching or his life, both of which of course inspired a million questions. I watched several times as El Duque spat out one-word answers to writers who rarely bothered to lift their pens. The language barrier actually made it easier for El Duque to conceal. The Yankees were not the United Nations; professional translators were not in great abundance. When the role fell to Cardenal, he often censored El Duque's answers for public consumption. "I wouldn't always translate everything he said," Cardenal told me. "I knew they were going to misinterpret it, so I wouldn't tell them everything."

No issue was more sensitive, of course, than the circumstances surrounding the great escape. From the moment El Duque arrived, he had been barraged with inevitable questions about his amazing journey, but the cover-up continued. El Duque didn't feel any moral misgivings; he believed that he was protecting the people who had returned to Cuba after delivering him to the Bahamas. But there was no way he could have imagined how wildly the story would spin out of control.

Controlling the Escape Story

In the original version cooked up in the Bahamas, . . . the group supposedly had traveled on a twenty-foot sailboat that took on water after leaving Cuba. The fictitious boat ultimately sank, stranding everyone on Anguilla Cay. Had El Duque then failed, had he languished in the minor leagues or ended up like Alberto Hernández, repairing cars in a Costa Rica garage or even toiling in obscurity for the Pittsburgh Pirates, no one would have given it a second thought. But a funny thing happened: El Duque became a rising star with the 1998 New York Yankees, one of the greatest teams ever assembled. And so his story, in the absence of real details, began to take on a life of its own.

El Duque's posturing only contributed to the growing-fish story. When he arrived in Tampa, he told the media that the escape was still too painful to discuss. In Columbus, he repeated this explanation whenever writers broached the subject. Then, after he was called up, he again said the matter was too painfull, his emotions too raw. . . .

Certainly, the story spun out of control. But at its core it was always a matter of loyalty to the people who had helped smuggle El Duque out of Cuba. Even [fellow escapee] Juan Carlos Romero, whose bitterness toward the pitcher was boundless, acknowledged that much. And the risks were real. Given El Duque's stature and the warnings issued by the Cuban government ("Stay out of Santa Clara!"), there was little question that the accomplices, had they been caught, would have been imprisoned.[2] For El Duque to declare publicly that the boat had gone back would have been tantamount to turning both of them in.

The story also took nothing away from what El Duque had accomplished. Most baseball players spend their off-season hunting and fishing. El Duque spent his fleeing an authoritarian government. In the span of ten months he had escaped Cuba on a fishing boat, survived four days on a deserted Bahamian island, spent another two days in a rat-infested refugee camp, pitched at a major-league tryout in San José, Costa Rica, signed a $6.6 million contract with the New York Yankees, then pitched his way onto one of the greatest teams in history.

2. Both eventually came to the United States but prefer to remain anonymous.

Chronology

1492
Christopher Columbus claims Cuba for Spain.

1868
Cuban citizens revolt against Spanish control, beginning the Ten Years' War.

1895
The war for independence begins.

1898
The United States joins Cuba in the Spanish-American War, which ends later in the same year.

1899
The United States installs a provisional military government in Cuba.

1901
The Platt Amendment is passed by Congress and accepted by Cuba, giving the United States authority to intervene in Cuban affairs.

1902
Tomás Estrada Palma is elected the first Cuban president, and Cuba officially becomes an independent republic, although the Platt Amendment remains in effect.

1933
General Fulgencio Batista, backed by the United States, establishes a dictatorship.

1934

The Platt Amendment is repealed after U.S. president Franklin D. Roosevelt negotiates a new treaty with Cuba.

1953

A young rebel, Fidel Castro, leads a failed coup attempt against Batista.

1959

Fidel Castro, along with fellow revolutionary Ernesto "Che" Guevara and a small band of guerrillas, overthrows the Batista government.

1960

President Castro allies Cuba with the Soviet Union, embraces communism, and severs ties with the United States, prompting tens of thousands of middle- and upper-class Cubans to flee to the United States.

1961

Approximately fourteen hundred CIA-trained Cuban exiles storm the beaches of Cuba, attempting to overthrow Castro in the failed Bay of Pigs invasion.

1962

The Cuban missile crisis provokes the specter of nuclear war.

1963

The U.S. trade embargo against Cuba, begun in 1962, is tightened, banning almost all travel to Cuba.

1965

The Freedom Flights program begins, which ultimately allows 250,000 Cubans to come to the United States.

1966

The Cuban Adjustment Act allows 123,000 Cubans to apply for permanent residence in the United States.

1975
The United States modifies its trade embargo to allow U.S. subsidiaries in foreign countries to trade with Cuba.

1977
The United States eases restrictions on travel to Cuba and allows Americans to spend one hundred dollars on Cuban goods while visiting the island.

1980
Fidel Castro allows more than 125,000 Cubans to leave for the United States in the Mariel Boat Lift.

1982
Charter air travel between the United States and Cuba is suspended, and monetary expenditures in Cuba are banned.

1985
U.S.-sponsored Radio Marti begins broadcasting in Cuba.

1991
The Soviet Union collapses, creating economic hardship in Cuba and forcing thousands of Cubans to try to escape to the United States.

1992
The United Nations condemns the U.S. embargo of Cuba.

1994
The United States and Cuba reach an agreement to allow twenty thousand Cuban immigrants into the United States each year.

1996
Four people are killed when two civilian aircraft, operated by Brothers to the Rescue, are shot down near Cuba while searching for Cuban raft people.

1999

Five-year-old refugee Elian Gonzalez is rescued from the sea.

2000

U.S. president Bill Clinton eases the decades-long embargo against Cuba.

2001

United States exports food to Cuba for the first time in more than forty years when Castro requests help after Hurricane Michelle.

2003

U.S. president George W. Bush once again tightens the embargo against Cuba, severely curtailing trade and visits to the island.

For Further Research

General Histories of Cuba

Alan Dye and Richard Sicotte, "The U.S. Sugar Program and the Cuban Revolution," *Journal of Economic History*, September 2004.

Carlos M.N. Eire, *Waiting for Snow in Havana*. New York: Free Press, 2003.

Andrea O'Reilly Herrera, ed., *Remembering Cuba: Legacy of a Diaspora*. Austin: University of Texas Press, 2001.

Orestes Lorenzo, *Wings of the Morning*. New York: St. Martin's, 1994.

John Miller and Aaron Kenedi, *Inside Cuba: The History, Culture and Politics of an Outlaw Nation*. New York: Marlowe, 2003.

Paul Rivero, "Life in Cuba," *Le Monde*, January 2, 1999.

Clifford Staten, *The History of Cuba*. Westport, CT: Greenwood, 2003.

Jaime Suchlicki, *Cuba: From Columbus to Castro*. New York: Scribner, 1974.

U.S. News & World Report, "Life in Cuba: 'I Was Like a Robot,'" April 28, 1980.

Cuban Immigrants: 1800s Through the Early 1960s

Richard H. Bradford, *The Virginius Affair*. Boulder: Colorado Associated University Press, 1980.

Brian Dooley, "The Cuban Missile Crisis—30 Years On," *History Today*, October 1992.

Evelio Grillo, *Black Cuban, Black American: A Memoir*. Houston, TX: Arte Publico, 2000.

Laura Hahn, *The Cuban Americans*. Philadelphia: Mason Crest, 2003.

Kenneth E. Hendrickson, *The Spanish American War*. Westport, CT: Greenwood, 2003.

Robert F. Kennedy, *Thirteen Days: A Memoir of the Cuban Missile Crisis*. New York: Norton, 1969.

George J.A. O'Toole, *The Spanish War: An American Epic—1898*. New York: Norton, 1984.

Gerald E. Poyo, *With All, and for the Good of All: The Emergence of Popular Nationalism in the Cuban Communities of the United States, 1848–1898*. Durham, NC: Duke University Press, 1989.

Liz Sonneborn, *The Cuban Americans*. San Diego: Lucent Books, 2002.

Victor Andres Triay, *The Bay of Pigs: An Oral History of Brigade 2506*. Gainesville: University Press of Florida, 2001.

Mark Weisenmiller, "Florida: Front-Line State in 1962," *History Today*, October 2002.

Modern Era: Culture and Politics

Thomas D. Boswell and Manuel Rivero, "Cubans in America: A Minority Group Comes of Age," *Focus*, April 1985.

Arian Campo-Flores, "Dance of the Cubans," *Newsweek*, March 10, 2003.

Carlos E. Cortes, ed., *The Cuban Experience in the United States*. New York: Arno, 1980.

Joan Didion, *Miami*. New York: Simon & Schuster, 1987.

Michael Duffy et al., "The Raid in Replay," *Time*, May 8, 2000.

Alfredo A. Fernandez, *Adrift: The Cuban Raft People*. Houston, TX: Arte Publico, 2000.

Gustavo Pérez Firmat, *Life on the Hyphen: The Cuban-American Way*. Austin: University of Texas Press, 1994.

Maria Cristina Garcia, *Havana USA: Cuban Exiles and Cuban Americans in South Florida, 1959–1994*. Berkeley: University of California Press, 1996.

Abraham F. Lowenthal, "From Bad to Worse on Cuba Policy," *San Diego Union-Tribune*, October 5, 2004.

John J. Miller, "Trouble in Miami," *National Review*, October 27, 2003.

Warren Richey, "Cuban Rafters May Exploit Asylum Loophole," *Christian Science Monitor*, May 11, 2000.

David Rieff, *Going to Miami*. Boston: Little, Brown, 1987.

David Savona, "An Interview with Carlos Toraño," *Cigar Aficionado*, November/December 2004.

Virgil Suarez, *Spared Angola: Memories from a Cuban American Childhood*. Houston, TX: Arte Publico, 1997.

Time, "The Flotilla Grows," May 12, 1980.

Web Sites

Bay of Pigs—Brigade 2506, www.brigada2506.com/index.html. Established to honor the members of Brigade 2506, this Web site includes a history of the Bay of Pigs invasion, information about the Bay of Pigs Museum and Library, and a gallery of photos of the men who perished during the invasion.

Cuban American National Foundation, www.canf.org. The CANF Web site offers detailed information about the history of the organization, news and opinion about

Cuba, and information about CANF activities and events.

Cuban Information Archives, http://cuban-exile.com/menu1/!refug.html. This site is an archive of information about Cuban immigrants to the United States. It includes a time line of significant immigration dates as well as links to several articles about the Cuban American experience.

The Spanish American War, www.loc.gov/rr/hispanic/1898. Resources and documents relating to the Spanish American War are provided on this Web site. It also includes an essay about Cuba during the war, maps, and a comprehensive chronology of Cuba in the years leading up to and including the war.

INDEX